SCIENTIFIC
POLICE
INVESTIGATION

Inbau Law Enforcement Series

SCIENTIFIC
POLICE
INVESTIGATION

FRED E. INBAU
Professor of Law, Northwestern University

ANDRE A. MOENSSENS
Associate Professor of Law,
Chicago-Kent College of Law,
Illinois Institute of
Technology

LOUIS R. VITULLO
Chief Microanalyst,
Criminalistics Division,
Chicago Police Department

CHILTON BOOK COMPANY

PHILADELPHIA   NEW YORK

To the memory of Newman F. Baker
F.E.I.

To my daughters, Monique, Jacqueline and Michele
A.A.M.

To my wife, Betty
L.R.V.

Preface

Every police officer knows that most crimes are solved by common sense and hard work. Many times, though, scientific techniques can be of considerable assistance, and occasionally they may be the only means by which to identify or to convict a criminal offender.

Police investigators all too often overlook the fact that, even after plain hard work has singled out the law breaker to their complete satisfaction, they may need to apply scientific techniques in order to secure the additional evidence necessary in court to establish proof of guilt "beyond a reasonable doubt." It is also tremendously helpful in many cases to assure the judge and jury that attempts have been made to utilize scientific techniques, even if to no avail. Under the mistaken impression that science can solve almost all criminal cases, jurors have been known to dismiss tight cases for "lack of evidence" —evidence that was not gathered scientifically enough, in their estimation. The following case exemplifies the problem.

A burglar prepared to rape the occupant of an apartment by making sure she couldn't see him. He unscrewed a light bulb. A suspect was later apprehended and was identified by the victim and by another person, who had seen him leave the apartment. He also had in his possession the same amount of money that was taken from the burglarized apartment. Yet the defendant was acquitted because no evidence was offered that his fingerprints were on the light bulb! The bulb had been dusted for fingerprints, but only smudges were revealed. The jury did not know that, and some of them remembered from mystery stories that such offenders always left fingerprints. Obviously, the use of scientific methods of criminal investigation is of utmost importance, and a jury should always be informed that the crime lab was involved in solving the case, even if its efforts were unproductive.

This book is not a textbook for specialists and experts. They have little or nothing to gain from it. Nor does it deal with criminal investigation generally—in terms of deductive reasoning processes and investigative tactics, interrogation, surveillance and the like. It addresses itself instead to the police officer who is summoned to the scene of a crime as the initial representative of the law. Its primary purpose is to make him aware of the existence and basic uses of the scientific aids that are most generally available; it also explains what he must look for and do in procuring and preserving the evidence that is to be subjected to scientific scrutiny.

Acknowledgments

We received much valuable assistance in the preparation of this book.

With regard to the chapter on document examination we were supplied with illustrations by the following examiners of questioned documents: Donald Doud of Chicago and Milwaukee, Ordway Hilton of New York City, Clark Sellers of Los Angeles and David J. Purtell of the Chicago Police Department. Mr. Doud and Captain Purtell also gave us helpful suggestions about the manuscript itself.

For their suggestions regarding the firearms identification chapter, we are indebted to Joseph D. Nicol of the University of Illinois (Chicago Circle) and John C. Stauffer of the Criminalistics Division of the Chicago Police Department.

Many of the illustrations for the chapter on tool mark identification, and many of the ideas embodied therein, were supplied by Arthur R. Paholke of the Criminalistics Division of the Chicago Police Department. Photographer Arthur W. Kleist, Jr., was also very cooperative in the preparation of a number of the photographs used in that and other chapters.

We extend our appreciation to the Director of the Criminalistics Division of the Chicago Police Department, Captain Francis J. Flanagan, for his cooperation in making the crime laboratory's facilities and personnel available to us.

Throughout the book are illustrations that were supplied by other persons for whom there are accompanying credit lines. To them, too, we are very grateful.

None of the above named individuals, or any others whose names appear in this book, should be faulted for whatever shortcomings the book may possess. That responsibility belongs to the authors alone.

F.E.I.
A.A.M.
L.R.V.

Contents

"Science is nothing but trained and organized common sense, differing from the latter only as a veteran may differ from a raw recruit; and its methods differ from those of common sense only so far as the guardsman's cut and thrust differ from the manner in which a savage wields his club."

Thomas H. Huxley in *Liberal Education*

Sherlock Holmes, expressing his concern about the destruction of valuable crime scene evidence by the police themselves, made this remark in *The Boscombe Valley Mystery:* "Oh, how simple it would all have been had I been here before they came like a herd of buffaloes and wallowed all over it."

SCIENTIFIC
POLICE
INVESTIGATION

Chapter 1

Photographs, Casts, Models, Maps and Diagrams

In order to convey ideas, we normally use a verbal description of what we seek to communicate. If we want to explain what type of car was involved in an accident, we can describe the car by make, model, year, color of body and interior, placement of radio antenna, license plates and other details. That is not too hard to do when a new car is involved because most people either have actually seen such a car or have seen reproductions of it. So it is fairly easy to build up a mental picture simply on the basis of a verbal description when that description agrees with a mental picture that was already formed. Things are different when we deal with an object or incident of which we know little or nothing. An automobile we are familiar with becomes involved in an accident, let's say, and is damaged. A verbal description of the dent in the fender and of the ripped-off side rear-view mirror may conjure up some mental picture, but it is not likely to be highly accurate. In order to convey what we have in mind accurately, some other means must be found. We can fully communicate the condition of the car by exhibiting it, showing the actual damage or showing photographs of it taken from several angles; we could even conceivably use a small model of the car with the damage to the original carefully imitated on the model.

But pictures do not eliminate the need for verbal description. The "picture," whether photograph, model or diagram, only assists the viewer in creating a mental image of actual conditions. Verbal description is still necessary, even indispensable. Showing a photograph or model of a damaged car has little meaning unless it is ac-

1

companied by a story of the circumstances under which the damage occurred. Yet its coverage of details is likely to be more inclusive, less given to omission, than a verbal description.

To show how attempts to paint a "picture" of details with words alone can easily be incomplete, we will conduct an often used experiment. Try to imagine a small kitchen with paper strewn everywhere, dirty kitchen utensils in the sink, garbage cans overflowing with a week's refuse, and filth in every corner. Now turn to Figure 1 and take a look at a photograph of such a scene. It is probably considerably different from the mental picture which the words alone evoked.

Photographs, models, maps or diagrams may be admitted as evidence in court only as *an adjunct to* verbal testimony—as "demonstrative evidence." In other words, a graphic representation cannot be used as courtroom evidence all by itself; it may be shown only because it assists the jury in better understanding the oral testimony of a witness. And since graphic representation is admissible only for the purpose of demonstrating and explaining what a witness is saying, someone must testify that the picture accurately portrays what it seems to show.

PHOTOGRAPHS

Photography provides probably the most potent tool in conveying facts to a jury. In law enforcement, however, photography plays an extremely important role in nearly every phase of the policeman's work. Invented in 1839 by Daguerre, photography was used as early as 1843 to provide pictures of arrested persons—what we now call "mug shots"—in Belgium. These early pictures were made on metal plates called daguerreotypes. The use of mug shots to identify individuals has survived to this day.

At a very early stage, photographs were also used to photograph scenes of crimes and accidents, of bodies and wounds, of suspect documents and checks, and of other items of evidence such as murder weapons. As photographic techniques became more sophisticated, still photographs of hairs, fibers, paint chips, tool marks and other minute items of trace evidence were made through a microscope. The advent of color photography, stereophotography, and infrared and ultraviolet picture taking, sometimes used in conjunction with a microscope, also permitted photographing small details that the human eye could not distinguish.

Because of the wide uses of photography by the public generally, it is probably the one type of evidence that is best understood by all people, including police officers, lawyers and judges. Almost everyone has used a simple camera, and a good many people can operate quite elaborate pieces of photographic equipment. All but the smallest law enforcement agencies possess photographic laboratories as well as a variety of specialized and general purpose photographic instruments.

Since photography is so widely used and provides the most accurate means for recording a maximum of information in the shortest possible time, it is important to understand at least the most basic principles.

Photographic Principles

Stripped of all the complexities designed to make the process of picture taking more efficient, a camera is essentially a light-tight box with an opening through which light can be admitted by the release of a shutter. If the shutter is opened, light entering the camera passes through the lens, which acts much like the human eye, and focuses on the back panel of the camera box. The back panel usually contains a window through which a portion of the film can be exposed to light and to the image that is to be photographed. Film comes in four types—sheet film, perforated, roll and film pack—and is basically a sheet of celluloid or glass that is ordinarily coated with an "emulsion" of smooth particles of silver halides suspended in gelatin. This emulsion is capable of retaining an invisible image upon exposure, because the silver salts are sensitive to light. When the shutter is opened to expose the film, the image that is being photographed fixes itself into these salts.

At that time, however, the image is still invisible, or latent. "Development" transforms the exposed silver halides into black metallic silver and fixes the image in place to produce a "negative"—the piece of film on which the image appears reversed and on which the light areas of the subject appear dark and the dark areas light. The development of the film must be done in a darkroom to prevent light from affecting the emulsion before the image is firmly fixed. After development, the film is usually passed through a "stop

Figure 1. Courtesy: Harris B. Tuttle, Sr.

bath," which simply arrests further development; then the film is placed in a "fixing bath," which removes all unexposed and undeveloped silver. After the film has passed through the fixing stage, the negative is no longer sensitive and can be viewed in daylight.

In order to obtain a photographic print on paper, a similar process is used. In contact printing, the emulsion (dull) side of the negative is placed against the emulsion side of photosensitized paper (coated with light-sensitive materials) and light is permitted to pass through the negative so that it reaches the sensitized paper. During this print-making process the technician may operate with a "safelight"—usually red or yellow—rather than in complete darkness. The image is then developed by passing the paper through a developer, a stop bath and a fixer. This process results in a "print" in which the image appears the same as it did when it was first viewed by the camera; that is, black areas in the subject matter again appear black in the print.

Often it is desired to enlarge the image appearing on the negative. This is done with the aid of an instrument called an enlarger, which is the reverse of a camera. Again, light passes through the negative to a lens, which projects the image on photosensitized paper, which is developed and fixed pretty much like contact prints. The enlargement may be adjusted to whatever scale desired.

In the manufacture of emulsions for film, several stages are involved. Each of these stages gives rise to special properties of the emulsion. Through the selection of proper combinations of stages and treatments, photographic emulsions of a distinct type can be manufactured. Emulsions can be prepared with selected sensitivity (orthochromatic, infrared, color) or emulsions may be sensitized to respond to the whole color spectrum in equal proportions (panchromatic).

Developing papers vary according to (1) type of emulsion (chloride, bromide, etc.), (2) contrast range (soft, hard, normal) and (3) physical properties (thickness, finish, color, texture, etc.). Most developing papers consist of silver chloride or silver bromide, or a combination of the two, which determines the sensitivity and image tone. Developing papers for color prints are usually of two types: positive and reversal. The positive paper is used to make color prints from color negatives, whereas the reversal paper is used to make color prints from color transparencies. Color developing papers are sensitized to blue, green and red light and contain complementary color couplers that record the colors of the negative.

Regardless of the characteristics of the film, developer and paper used, the appearance of the final picture may still be affected by the use of filters, either on the camera or during development; in fact, it can be affected even by the length of time of exposure or development or by the use of a great number of compensating factors such as reducers or intensifiers. The degree of accuracy with which the picture portrays the original can be affected by a number of other factors as well.

Police Photography

All of these considerations point to the need for police photographers who are highly skilled in their field and who have a thorough understanding of cameras, lenses, light-sensitive materials, processing chemicals and the like. In the final analysis, however, "police photography" is not a branch of photography which requires extensive training; any skilled professional photographer or advanced amateur can do police photography work once he has been instructed in its special requirements. In fact, amateur photographers often know as much about it as the "pros" and are distinguished from them only in that their equipment is probably less costly and photography is not their occupation.

Police photographs of individuals, crime scenes, accidents and trace evidence must be absolutely honest and stark. The prime directive is to produce a photograph that accurately portrays the person or subject photographed. Commercial photography, on the other hand, seeks to enhance certain details in a picture through the use of special lenses, sensitive materials, filters, lighting and so forth. If the desired effect is not achieved to the satisfaction of a commercial photographer, he can retouch either the negative or the enlargement. No enhancement or retouching of any kind is permitted in photographs taken of crime scenes or for personal identification.

Crime scene photography and mug shots are only two of the areas with which police photographers are concerned. They also have to assist in the photographic needs of all the other specialists in scientific crime detection. Almost every phase of criminalistics depends to a large extent on photography for investigation, analysis or demonstration. The fingerprint expert requires photographs of latent impressions, inked impressions or court exhibits. So does the examiner of questioned documents. Both of these specialists, and others as well, may require the use of special techniques to make evidence visible that may otherwise be poorly discernible or invisible to the naked eye.

The use of infrared light-sensitive emulsions or ultraviolet lighting may produce evidence of fine detail that is invisible to the eye, as in documents altered by erasures, overwritings or tracings. X-ray photography may reveal the presence of a bullet and its precise location inside such objects as door jambs or the wooden post of a table (see Figure 2), as well as the presence of lead in loaded dice. The application of the microscope to photography, in order to produce photomicrographs, may show detail that is too refined to be visible without the use of the great magnification provided by such optical equipment.

Many specialists in particular fields of criminalistics are also competent photographers in their own right, at least insofar as their field of specialty requires, but the competent police photographer is familiar with the special procedures and advanced techniques of all areas of criminalistics.

The extensive use of photographs of crime scenes permits one to

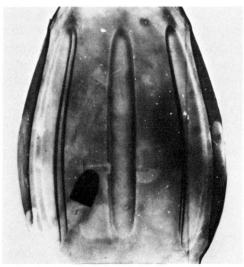

Figure 2.

present, in pictorial form, all of the facts and physical circumstances of a case; it aids in preserving available evidence; it permits the consideration of certain types of evidence that because of their size or form cannot be brought into court easily; it permits reconstruction of past events at some later date; and generally it assists in accurately revealing the conditions prevailing at a past event. In addition, a good photographic record also reveals physical evidence that might otherwise be easily overlooked and constitutes an excellent refresher for the investigator when he must testify in court about some event that happened months earlier.

A crime scene should be photographed as soon as possible because the longer the delay, the greater the likelihood that some changes may be made that would reflect on the accuracy of the crime scene photograph. Before anything is touched or moved, therefore, the investigator should complement his own observations and notes by making a photographic record of the entire area, viewed from every conceivable angle, with close-up photographs of all objects or items that may play an important role in solving the crime. Whenever possible, crime scene photographs should not include officers or observers.

It may sometimes be necessary to draw particular attention to a small area in a large room to show its relationship to other subjects before a close-up photograph is taken. If this is necessary, two photographs should be taken, one with a marker (such as a paper arrow) and one without. Some courts might refuse to admit into evidence a photograph that contains extraneous items not present at the crime scene, including such a marker. It is always better, therefore, to make more photographs than are thought to be needed; the cost involved is relatively slight and once the scene is disturbed it may be impossible to go back and take additional pictures.

Whenever violent deaths are involved, photographs of the crime scene should include the body. The victim should be photographed from all angles to show his or her relationship to other articles in the area and also to enable identification of the victim. If any wounds or marks are visible on the body, close-ups are also necessary.

The crime scene includes the whole area surrounding the place where the criminal act occurred. If a crime was committed in one room inside an apartment, adjoining rooms must be photographed as well. The building itself should be photographed, including close-ups of places where the perpetrator might have gained access, such as windows or doors. In addition, suspect tire marks or foot impressions should be recorded photographically. In certain instances, aerial photographs of the general crime scene can be very helpful.

During this whole process, the photographer must keep a careful record of each photograph taken, including details concerning date, time, other officers present, location described with particularity, type of film, camera and lens used, exposure, lens opening and any other relevant information. After development and printing, the photographer will be able to complement the photographic record with information about the types of chemicals, paper and equipment used in the darkroom. All of this information must ultimately be marked on the back of each photographic print or enlargement, as well as on the envelope containing the negatives. The negatives should also preferably contain a number referring to the case, either written or stamped in a corner so that it does not interfere with or obliterate parts of the negative image. All negatives should be preserved, even those that "did not come out" because of faulty exposure or other circumstances. Since properly taken color photographs convey more accurate information than black-and-white photographs, color film should be used whenever possible or practical.

Special Photographic Techniques

As the most powerful tool in the arsenal of the scientific crime investigator because of its wide range of applications, photography can be used or misused to produce misleading evidence—misleading in the sense that the pictures may be made to appear different from what the eye observed. We have just said that in crime scene photography absolute honesty of reproduction is required and retouching is prohibited. In the crime laboratory, though, it is sometimes necessary to call on special photographic techniques in order to render visible details that can be recorded by a camera but are invisible to the naked eye. A great number of these special processes are available. The selection of the one that is best suited for a particular job depends upon the type of evidence involved and the result sought. A few of the most important techniques can be discussed briefly here.

Filters

Filters are usually made up of colored discs of glass or gelatine. They stop some light, which means that the color of the light that passes through any filter is changed. Filters are used to correct color, to brighten or darken colors for certain effects, to change the color temperature of light in color photography, and to enable pictures to be taken by light of a single color. They are also used in photography with polarized light.

Sunlight, which is usually referred to as white light, is actually made up of rays of light composed of all the colors in the rainbow in exactly the same proportions as they appear there. The rainbow constitutes the visible spectrum of light. When it is broken down into its components—by being passed through a crystal, for example—the colors range from red on one side of the spectrum to violet on the other side. In between are orange, yellow, green and blue.

So by the proper use of filters it becomes possible to emphasize some colors and suppress others. When the color of a filter is the same as one of the colors in the image, that color will turn out lighter in the photograph than it actually is, and the colors of the opposite side of the spectrum will appear to be darker in the photograph. Considering that black-and-white photographs depict a scene in varying shades of gray, a red object may be made to ap-

pear to be quite light in a black-and-white photograph by placing a
red filter over the lens. By contrast, blue objects are made to appear
to be dark or even black when a red filter is used. A blue filter
would lighten a blue object but would also make any red portions
of it appear to be black or dark gray. This happens only, of course,
if the type of film used is one that records all colors in the same degree as the human eye sees them—panchromatic film. Some films
are made with emulsions that are not able to "see" certain colors,
such as orthochromatic film which does not register red light. A red
object photographed on orthochromatic film will therefore appear
black or dark in the photograph even though no filters were used.

In the crime laboratory, then, filters can be of great value when it
is necessary to either lighten or darken certain portions of a photograph, a process referred to as "varying the contrast." This is well illustrated in the two pictures shown in Figure 3. On the left is a
photograph of a postage stamp as it appeared to the naked eye,
nearly obliterated by heavy, red pencil marks. The photograph was
taken without a filter on regular (panchromatic) film. On the right
is a photograph of the same postage stamp, but this time a red filter
was placed over the lens, and that lightened the red pencil marks so
much that they are hardly visible. This procedure revealed that the
stamp had been previously used and cancelled by the post office.

The use of filters to alter the contrast is of great importance to
both the fingerprint technician and the questioned document examiner. The fingerprint technician may use it to photograph a latent

Figure 3. Courtesy: Institute of Applied Science

fingerprint developed on a multicolored surface, such as a magazine cover. By using a filter of essentially the same color as the background (magazine cover illustration), he can make that background appear to be white or light gray, so that the fingerprint developed with black powder stands out more clearly and can be studied with greater ease.

The document examiner, too, has frequent use for contrast filters, as when it comes to photographing endorsement signatures on cancelled checks. Blue or red bank stamps are often placed over portions of signatures, making it difficult to study the fine detail of the handwriting. By using contrasting filters to blot out (lighten) such stamps, a photograph may be produced which makes the check appear as if it were free from stamps. In that fashion, the examiner can properly examine all of the fine detail of the signatures.

Other types of filters may at times be used, not always to vary tonal quality, but to correct the image that would be imperfectly recorded on the film if no filters were used. This is particularly true of color photographs taken under artificial lighting. Considering that not all light sources emit light rays that have the qualities of sunlight—that is, a combination, in equal proportions, of all the colors of the rainbow—it may sometimes be necessary to compensate for deficiencies in available light by using filters that will render colors accurately.

There are also "neutral density filters," which absorb an equal percentage of all colors. This requirement is desirable for taking photographs in bright sunlight with a high-speed film. The camera may not be equipped with a fast enough shutter or a small enough lens opening, or both, to prevent overexposure. Using a neutral density filter reduces the intensity of the light striking the film so that a normally exposed photograph can be obtained.

Polarizing filters are used in both black-and-white and color photography to eliminate unwanted reflections of stray light, such as are produced when the light source is reflected from glass, polished metal or other highly reflective surfaces. The use of a polarizing screen in color photography can assist in increasing color saturation.

Infrared Photography

In our discussion on filters, we talked about the visible spectrum of light and stated that sunlight is made up of a combination, in equal proportions, of rays of light of all the colors of the rainbow. It is the wavelength of a ray of light that determines its color. In the visible spectrum, red rays have the longest wavelength and violet rays have the shortest. There are various ways of expressing wavelengths—in millimeters, centimeters, cycles, kilocycles—depending upon the types of radiation.

The visible spectrum is but a small part of a much broader whole, the electromagnetic spectrum, which includes alternating current on the one extreme (very long waves) and cosmic rays on the other (extremely short waves). In between we find ordinary radio waves near the longwave end of the electromagnetic spectrum, and X rays and gamma rays near the shortwave end. Visible light, then, differs from other types of radiation only in the length of the waves. Figure 4 shows the electromagnetic spectrum with wavelengths expressed in mathematical units.

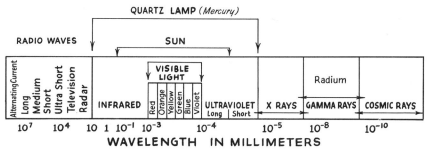

Figure 4. The Electromagnetic Spectrum.

At the longwave end of the visible spectrum there exists a band of radiation waves called infrared waves. One of the characteristics of infrared waves is that they are readily absorbed and converted into heat energy. But they are not heat waves. The radiant energy felt as heat is a result of molecular thermal agitation, which is a surface phenomenon of a hot object, such as a lamp filament, emitting rays. Any object that gives off electromagnetic radiation gives off some waves in the infrared region as long as the object has a temperature above absolute zero. The temperature of the object determines the quantity of infrared radiation. The hotter an object is, the more infrared waves are emitted.

Infrared waves cannot be seen by the human eye and they are not actually red. The word "infrared" indicates that type of radiation which adjoins the red rays of the visible spectrum. While infrared radiation cannot be "seen" by the human eye, photographic emulsions can be made that are sensitive to them. And that is what makes infrared radiation particularly useful to the criminalist, especially to the examiner of questioned documents.

Since most infrared plates or films are also sensitive to the visible portions of the spectrum, it is customary to use a filter on the camera lens that screens out all visible light but permits the infrared "picture" to pass and be recorded. In that fashion, a photographer may be able to discover erasures on documents, and sometimes he can even reveal what was originally written underneath other words. Infrared photography can also distinguish among inks and reveal blood stains and powder burns on cloth and clothing. Snooperscopes and hidden camers equipped with infrared lenses are used to observe people in the dark and to photograph intruders.

Ultraviolet Photography

Immediately outside the other end of the visible light spectrum is the ultraviolet band (see again Figure 4). Since this band occupies quite a wide spread of wavelengths, it is divided into shortwave and longwave ultraviolet rays. The longwave ultraviolet rays lie next to the visible light spectrum; the shortwave rays are closer to the X-ray band.

Because it emits rays in the invisible region of the electromagnetic spectrum, ultraviolet light is often referred to as black light, although more technically the term "black light" is limited to the longer wave ultraviolet rays. The usefulness of ultraviolet light in criminalistics stems from the fact that many substances fluoresce or give off visible light when exposed to ultraviolet rays. This fluorescence occurs because such substances have the power to receive radiant energy of a certain (invisible) wavelength and to convert portions of that energy into a longer wavelength within the visible light range, resulting in a visible glow that can be clearly seen when all ordinary visible light is blocked off, as in a darkened area.

A frequent use of ultraviolet light in crime detection is in the identification of people who have committed petty thefts. There are a great number of powders that fluoresce, and they come in many colors. Some are green; some are a buff color approximating the color of the skin. When thefts occur in offices, plants or schools, some of the powder can be placed in the coat pockets or money boxes from which thefts have occurred. This powder is so tenacious that even a vigorous washing of the hands will not immediately remove all traces of it. By requesting suspects to pass their hands under an ultraviolet lamp, officials can detect the guilty.

Invisible crayons and pens permit the secret marking of money, works of art and other valuables for easy identification, and, in the intelligence field, the writing of secret messages between the lines of seemingly innocuous letters. Using fluorescent powder on multi-colored surfaces that are dusted for fingerprints may render them visible under ultraviolet light without distracting backgrounds. Bodily secretions such as urine, semen, perspiration and pus often glow when illuminated with ultraviolet rays, thus permitting the detection of otherwise invisible traces on clothing. In the questioned document field, again, obliterated writings can often be rendered visible by exposure to ultraviolet rays.

Unlike infrared photography, ultraviolet photography does not require specially prepared emulsions because most panchromatic films are sensitive to ultraviolet radiation as well as to visible light. Any light source that emits ultraviolet rays will do for ultraviolet photography. A quartz lamp with a filter over the lens screening out all infrared and visible light rays is all that is needed in addition to standard photographic equipment.

X-ray Photography

In addition to the infrared and ultraviolet bands of the electromagnetic spectrum, a third band of rays can be useful in police work. But X-ray photography requires special generating equipment: a vacuum tube through which an electric current is passed is needed to produce X rays that can affect photographic plates.

X rays have the property of being able to penetrate objects that appear to be opaque to the naked eye. If an object is placed between a photographic plate and a source of X-ray emission, the photographic plate will record, in varying degrees of black and white, the density of the object. The densest objects appear white; the least dense, black. A reversed-density print made from an X-ray film was illustrated earlier in Figure 2, showing a bullet lodged inside the wooden leg of a table.

Photomicrography

Microscopic vision differs from photographic enlargement in that through a microscope we see a small area of an object greatly enlarged, whereas a photographic enlargement results in a magnification of a complete object, not just a small portion of it. When a camera is fitted to a microscope and an object is filmed, the result is called a photomicrograph. Examples of such photomicrographs and the uses of this technique in criminalistics are illustrated in the chapters on firearms identification, and comparative micrography and microanalysis. Most cameras can be fitted to take photographs through a microscope, although some require special attachments.

Photomacrography

This is the photographing of an object at initial magnification on the negative without the use of a microscope. In photomicrography, remember, the enlargement on the negative is obtained by shooting through a microscope. In photomacrography, only the camera or a special lens is used to obtain a detailed view on the negative which appears there larger than it does in actuality. This may be done by the use of extension bellows on certain press cameras, view cameras or other specially designed professional cameras. For practical reasons, the initial magnification in photomacrography is limited to fifty power. To obtain a greater initial enlargement, it is generally necessary to utilize a microscope in connection with the camera.

The Admissibility of Photographs and Film as Evidence

Before photographs may be admitted in court a "foundation" must be laid. This consists essentially of testimony properly identifying each photograph and establishing that it accurately portrays what it appears to show. Such testimony need not be furnished by the photographer himself; most courts permit any credible witness who can, from his own knowledge, authenticate the photograph and vouch for its accuracy to establish the foundation of truthfulness. The credible witness is usually the investigating police officer who first arrived at the crime scene and who perhaps also witnessed the photography. Testimony with respect to the accuracy of the photographic evidence should not be taken lightly, since it is often challenged on cross-examination.

The effects of various photographic devices and accessories on a picture sometimes appear to distort the scene it depicts. A room shot through a wide-angle lens, for example, can appear to be larger or roomier than it really is. Conversely, a telephoto lens causes an object in a photograph to appear to be much closer to the camera than it would appear to a viewer looking at the object from the point where the photograph was taken.

Other real or apparent distortions can be obtained by very simple techniques that do not involve retouching or altering the negative. A dramatic illustration is provided in Figure 5, which appears to depict a road at the crest of a mountain ridge. Actually, this photograph is printed upside down. By turning the book upside down the correct impression is conveyed, namely that of a river (the Snake River) flowing through canyons. It is obvious, then, that not-

Figure 5.

ing the type of lens used as well as all other relevant information concerning the taking of the photograph can be crucial in preparing photographic evidence.

Color Photographs and Slides

Black-and-white photographs were first admitted in court cases as early as 1859. Since then, courts have freely permitted them, provided that the requirements of proper foundation, relevancy and materiality are met. But even though the Eastman Kodak Company started distributing Kodachrome film in 1935, the question of the admissibility of color photographs was not decided until 1943, when a court held that color pictures are admissible under the same rules that govern the admissibility of black-and-white photographs.

Courts no longer distinguish between black-and-white and color photographs when it comes to deciding on admissibility. Photographs may be ruled inadmissible when they are highly inflammatory and gruesome, though, and therefore likely to inflame jurors. This is more likely to occur with color photographs that show a lot of blood on or around a victim, but the mere fact that a photograph is gruesome does not by itself make it inadmissible. The courts ordinarily say that a photograph becomes inadmissible when its inflammatory effect outweighs whatever evidential value it might have. A similar approach has been taken by the courts in connection with the admissibility of color slides that are to be projected onto a screen in court.

Color photographs clearly give a jury a better understanding of the issues than they might get from black-and-white photographs. In fact, it is frequently stated that if color photography had been invented before black-and-white photography it would be next to impossible to get a court to admit a black-and-white photograph: without colors, it would be said to portray its subject inaccurately because everyone with normal vision sees things in color.

Motion Pictures and Videotape

The filming of persons arrested for committing crimes has been particularly useful in cases that involve intoxicated drivers, probably because of the difficulty of obtaining convictions in such cases by means of other evidence of intoxication alone. When the prosecution is based solely on an officer's testimony regarding the physical appearance of a defendant at the time of the offense and his inability to perform simple tests such as walking a straight line and picking up coins scattered over the floor, the rate of conviction is extremely low. Juries, demanded by defendants, are made up of ordinary people who may themselves be social drinkers and are usually reluctant to convict a defendant who, days, weeks or months after his alleged offense, appears in court well dressed, clean shaven, behaving quite gentlemanly and looking very much like the jurors do. They have difficulty picturing such a defendant as a man with disarranged clothing, unzippered fly and bloodshot eyes, stumbling around in a disoriented manner, as the police officer has described him. Even a photograph such as the one shown in

Figure 6 (posed) does not convey the message as well as a movie or videotape can.

The advent of chemical testing for intoxication helped but did not completely solve the problem of low conviction rate. Expert testimony concerning the alcohol content of the defendant's blood, based on analysis of the blood, breath or urine, tended to lend added weight to the prosecution's case, especially in view of the fact that many states enacted laws defining levels of presumed intoxication based on blood-alcohol percentages. Over all, however, the conviction rate still remained fairly low, rising from 0–5% to about 30–40%.

It was this state of affairs which prompted some progressive de-

Figure 6.

partments to adopt the practice of making motion pictures of persons arrested on drunken driving charges. Started in Fresno, California, about 1945 with an amateur 8mm camera, the practice spread fairly rapidly. Today, a number of departments have color-sound motion-picture cameras with which they record the condition, behavior and speech of persons arrested for driving while intoxicated. The adoption of this technique has resulted in a dramatic increase in the conviction rate, up to 85–95% in many places. Most of these convictions are obtained on guilty pleas after a private viewing of the film by the defendant's attorney.

A few departments are using videotape as a substitute for sound motion pictures and record the same success in obtaining convictions. Videotape differs from movies in that the picture and sound are recorded on magnetic tape rather than on film. Other uses have been found for motion pictures and videotape as well, especially in recent years. Some departments have made use of them to film reenactments of crimes; others have filmed confessions so as to have proof that the proper warnings of constitutional rights were given and that the confession was voluntarily made, that is, without undue influence or coercion.

A few additional factors are to be considered with respect to sound motion pictures. The sound track of a movie can be made in two ways. The first method employs the use of a magnetic tape or wire recorder. In this process, the audio portion of the movie is separately recorded and later magnetically transferred to the film strip. Tapes or wires that are prepared in this manner can be altered or cut almost without detection and certainly without affecting the visual portion of the film. For that reason, a number of courts have held that such sound movies are inadmissible.

The second process by which the audio portion of a movie can be recorded is through the use of optical recording; that is, a device on the camera transforms the sound into optical patterns and records them directly on the film alongside the visual portion. Since optical sound records cannot be erased or modified, motion pictures making use of this process have been freely admitted, provided the other requirements for admissibility are met. These other requirements include some expanded form of testimony on authenticity. Because of the greater possibility of exaggeration by control of camera speed and editing, courts often require testimony to establish the following facts:

1. The circumstances surrounding the taking of the film, including the competence of the cameraman, the types of camera, film and lens, weather conditions or lighting arrangements, and the speed at which the film was taken.
2. The manner and circumstances surrounding the development of the film, including proper chain-of-custody evidence.
3. The manner of film projection, including the speed of projection and the distance of the projector from the screen.
4. Testimony by someone who was present at the time the film was taken to establish the accuracy with which the filmed scene depicts the actual events that were filmed.

Together, these requirements establish that the motion picture presents a true and accurate reproduction of the scene or event.

The courts have generally held that the same rules of evidence which govern the admissibility of still photographs apply to motion pictures, since they consider movies to consist of a series of still pictures.

While little court authority exists with respect to the admissibility of videotape, it may be expected that the courts will generally take the same approach as they have taken with respect to sound motion pictures.

CASTS, MODELS, MAPS AND DIAGRAMS

Casts

Rather than introducing photographic evidence, or in addition to it, it is often useful to use in court three-dimensional representations of an object. The best-known item of evidence in this category is the plaster cast or mold. It consists essentially of a reproduction, in plaster or some other substance, of an imprint that is discovered at a crime scene. Such an imprint may be a tire impression in mud or wet soil, a shoe impression, or an imprint of any other type of object which contains characteristic marks.

Certain plastics, resins and materials used by dentists for mouth impressions for dentures are other materials that can be used to make casts and models. Especially useful is a 2-to-1 mixture of paraffin and rosin for making casts in loose materials such as sand. The selection of the casting material should be determined by the circumstances.

Plaster casts are relatively easy to make, provided a good grade of plaster is used and the investigator has some experience in working with it. The plaster is mixed in water until it becomes creamy. It is then poured over the entire surface to a thickness of about ½ inch. At that time, some reinforcing wire or sticks are added, after which more plaster is poured into the mold. After the plaster has set, a process that does not ordinarily take more than 15 or 20 minutes, the cast can be removed. It must then be carefully washed in water or under a low-pressure stream. The investigator must also carefully mark the back side of the cast as to the place where taken, on what date, by whom and so forth.

Special techniques may be needed when the impression is in sand, loose soil or even snow because ordinary pouring of the wet plaster may destroy fine characteristic detail of the imprint. Among these techniques are strengthening of the marks with a plastic spray, shellac or other quick-drying fixative. Before any attempt is made to make a plaster cast of an imprint, the trace should be photographed in case the imprint detail is obliterated by the casting process.

Models

Another type of demonstrative evidence that is sometimes prepared consists of a scale model of a place or building, to be utilized in court in order to permit the jury to more clearly understand where and how a crime was committed. One outstanding example of such a model was used in a recent case in Illinois. Eight nurses had been murdered in a townhouse. In preparation for the trial of the accused killer, the prosecution had a scale model fabricated of the townhouse where the girls lived and where the crime occurred. Figure 7 shows how this model appeared. It is of course extremely important that the model be made exactly to scale, which calls for accurate measurements and great skill in building miniature details.

Maps and Diagrams

Another supplement to photography is the use of maps, diagrams and sketches. While it is necessary to record, photographically, all of the detail of a crime scene, photographs still miss some important data that cannot be effectively transmitted unless sketches or diagrams are also used. The room where a homicide occurs appears, when viewing photographs, as a series of overlapping photographs. Only a detailed sketch, with all dimensions accurately marked or

Figure 7.

drawn to scale, can give an overall view of the room layout. Such a sketch is shown in Figure 8, a drawing of a summer cottage where a homicide occurred. Photographs of that one-room cottage could show what type of furniture was present, how high the windows were but the overall relationship of these items to the total area could best be shown in a drawing of the locale.

Even a drawing of a building might not be completely satisfactory: it may need to be supplemented by a sketch of the building in relation to the street, the paths through the garden, the location of a garage or shed, and the location of trees and shrubbery that might have made it impossible to observe from the street what happened inside or which might have provided shelter for the criminal as he left the premises. Again, photographs can accurately record details of the surrounding location and views from certain directions, but it is only when a map of the entire surroundings is drawn that everything can be viewed in its true perspective.

In automobile accident cases, photographs are extremely important, but just as important is a sketch of the precise location of the vehicle(s) in relation to the curb, the intersection, the center of the road or the traffic signs. Drawings and sketches, then, as well as maps, must record the exact location and relationship of all of the important pieces of evidence at the crime scene. This does not require special talent as a draftsman or artist, and any officer can learn to do this if he only takes the time to record accurate measurements.

It is sometimes useful to use professionally drawn maps of certain

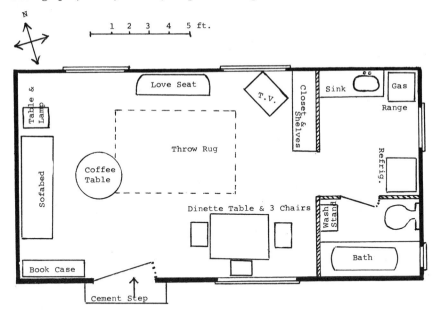

SUMMER COTTAGE AT 13843 BUTTERNUT LANE, FOX RIVER GROVE, ILL.

Figure 8.

districts or towns, particularly when a criminal is reported to have traveled from one location to another, and then again to a third location, or when it becomes necessary to explain exactly what routes he followed and how long it took him to visit the different locales. Such maps may be obtained from various city departments, since they are used to assist in traffic planning, designing zoning areas, laying out and repairing sewage and utility lines, or dividing areas into school districts, election precincts or census tracks. Larger cities have a special department of cartography which prepares such maps, and specialists can be borrowed from that department.

The admission into evidence of diagrams, maps and sketches is generally within the discretion of the trial judge. His decision to admit or exclude such evidence is not ordinarily disturbed on appeal unless a clear abuse of discretion is shown. The fact that drawings are not exactly to scale does not make them inadmissible per se, although it might have an effect on the judge's decision. Testimony given on the basis of an official map might be admitted as an official document, without the necessity of calling as a witness the individual who drew the map or the head of the office who supervised the drawing of maps. Then, too, if an officer or other person checks the street measurements and other things shown on the map and thus verifies its accuracy, his testimony alone can authenticate the map for courtroom purposes.

REFERENCES

Anon., *Basic Police Photography*, 2nd ed., Eastman Kodak Company (Rochester), 1964.

Anon., *Encyclopedia of Photography*, Greystone Press (New York), 1964.

Baines, *The Science of Photography*, rev. ed., John Wiley & Sons (New York), 1967.

Chernoff and Sarbin, *Photography and the Law*, American Photographic Book Publishing Company (New York), 1958.

Cox, *Photographic Optics*, 13th ed., Focal Press (New York), 1966.

Langford, *Basic Photography*, Focal Press (New York), 1965.

Newhall, *The History of Photography*, rev. ed., Museum of Modern Art (New York), 1964.

Sansone, *Modern Photography for Police and Firemen*, W. H. Anderson Company (Cincinnati), 1971.

Scott, *Photographic Evidence*, 3 vols., 2nd ed., West Publishing Company (St. Paul), 1969.

Chapter 2

Fingerprint Identification

Fingerprints have been used as "sign manuals" or in lieu of signatures for a long time. Modern usage as a means of establishing an individual's identity, however, is less than a century old.

Around 1860, William Herschel, a British colonial civil servant in India, started the practice of imprinting the handprints of natives on their contracts to prevent the impersonation and refutation of signatures. This experiment lead to Herschel's further limited inquiries in the use of fingerprints, but he never developed a workable system that could be practically applied.

Working independently on the same problem, Henry Faulds, a Scottish doctor and medical missionary in Japan, was the first to write, in 1881, that the identity of a criminal could be established by means of the finger impressions he left at the crime scene; and the first textbook on fingerprinting was authored by Sir Francis Galton in 1892. Galton had taken up and expanded Herschel's studies. As a result of Galton's efforts, some limited use was made of fingerprints between the date of publication of his book and the official adoption of fingerprinting at Scotland Yard right after the turn of the century.

Meanwhile, a French policeman, Alphonse Bertillon, had developed a system of personal identification by bodily measurements which had gained swift popularity in Europe and in the United States during the 1880s. The system was called "anthropometry," but it was popularly referred to as the "Bertillon system," just as the early identification officers came to be referred to as "Bertillon officers." This name lingered on even after the unreliable features of

25

anthropometry had been exposed and the superiority of fingerprinting had been established as a reliable means of personal identification. So ingrained was the use of the term "Bertillon officers" to designate identification men that to this day some policemen and laymen alike still refer to Bertillon as the "inventor" of fingerprinting, although he had nothing to do with its actual development as a means of identification. In fact, he opposed its introduction in France until his death, except as an adjunct to the anthropometrical files.

Fingerprinting came into widespread use in the United States from about 1910 on, after some isolated experiments on a local level, started in 1902, proved successful. Today, all moderate to large law enforcement agencies have fingerprint identification bureaus. Some are independent units within departments; others are parts of crime laboratories. Most states also have statewide identification agencies, often as part of a department of public safety, a department of corrections or the attorney general's office. The largest collection of fingerprints in the world is housed in the Federal Bureau of Investigation in Washington, D.C.

Fingerprinting has many uses other than those to which it is put in the criminal justice processes. Fingerprints have been used in the place of signatures on wills and contracts made by illiterates. Another frequent and valuable noncriminal use is in the identification of deceased victims of airplane crashes and other disaster victims whose bodies are sometimes so badly mutilated that visual identification is not possible.

SCOPE AND FUNDAMENTAL PRINCIPLES

A fingerprint is a reproduction of the intricate design of friction skin ridges found on the palm side of a finger or thumb. The same type of friction skin can also be found on the whole palmar surface of the hands and on the plantar surfaces (soles) of the feet. There is no physical, physiological or biological difference between the friction skin on the fingers and that on the palms of the hands and the soles of the feet.

The friction skin ridges bear rows of sweat pores through which perspiration is exuded. The perspiration acts as a lubricant of the skin. Because of this perspiration, and the incidental coating of the skin with bodily oils, an impression of the ridge pattern of the finger is left whenever the finger touches a smooth surface. Such an impression is called a "latent print." It is usually invisible to the naked eye but can be made to appear through the proper use of fingerprint powders, vapors or chemical solutions. Some impressions left in colored substances such as blood or paint are clearly visible without developing procedures. Others are of a plastic, or embossed, nature, such as those impressed in putty, grease, wax or mud. While a distinction is sometimes made between invisible, visible and embossed impressions, most fingerprint technicians refer to all accidentally left impressions as latent prints.

The practical uses in law enforcement of a system of fingerprint identification derive from three well-established premises: (1) the friction ridge patterns begin to develop during fetal life (before birth), remain unchanged during life and even after death until decomposition of the body destroys the ridged skin; (2) the patterns differ from individual to individual, and even from digit to digit, and are never duplicated in their minute details; (3) although all patterns are distinct in their ridge characteristics, their overall pattern appearance shows similarities that can be used to permit systematic classification of the impression into well-defined classes.

From childhood to maturity, the friction skin patterns expand in size. As an adult grows old, they may also shrink in size. The characteristic points of the prints which are used to determine their individuality, however, do not undergo any natural change during lifetime. Rare cases of mutilation, accidental or intentional, or the occurrence of some skin disease such as leprosy, may partially or totally destroy the skin ridges. But if the destruction is only partial, it will not affect the value of the impressions for identification purposes because complete patterns are not needed.

The ridges that are visible on the palm side of a finger are those that are formed on the outer layer of the skin, called the epidermis. These patterned ridges are formed through a process of differential growth in the dermis (under layer) of the skin, where a pattern develops that is absolutely identical to those visible on the epidermis. If the finger is superficially hurt or mutilated, a temporary scar will appear, but after the injury heals the pattern will grow back exactly as it was before because the epidermis regenerates itself over the dermal pattern. If the injury inflicted is deeper than approximately one millimeter and reaches into the dermis of the skin to damage the ridge-molding "dermal papillae," a permanent scar will remain on the outer skin after the healing process is completed. As long as sufficient undamaged skin remains on the finger, however, identification by its impression will not be impaired.

When a person is arrested by the police, his fingerprints are recorded on standard 8 x 8-inch fingerprint cards. One such card is illustrated in Figure 9. The fingers are rolled one by one over an inked slab and then onto the fingerprint card in the proper spaces that are provided for each finger and thumb. In addition to the spaces for rolled impressions, the bottom half of the card also has spaces for plain impressions, made by pressing down the four fingers and the thumb without a rolling motion. The fingerprints taken upon arrest are usually taken in triplicate by local law enforcement agencies. One copy is kept for the agency's files, one is sent to the state identification bureau, and another is sent to the FBI.

After the impressions have been recorded, the cards are sent to the agency's identification bureau for classifying, searching and filing. The first process involves assigning to the card a classification formula that is based on a study of the general types of patterns and their subdivisions. After the card has been classified, the files are searched by the classification formula to determine whether the person has been previously fingerprinted and, if so, on what occasion. In that manner it can be established whether the individual has a prior record. Since the search is by fingerprint classification rather than by name of the individual, it will also reveal the fact that on a prior arrest the individual had used a different name or alias. If the search does not turn up a prior record card for the person, his card is filed in the appropriate place in the files for future reference.

After latent impressions found at the scene of a crime have been rendered visible, they may be compared with the impressions on file. Thus, by means of fingerprints alone and without any other leads or clues, the police may be able to discover the identity of the person leaving the latent fingerprints at an incriminating location.

A very important fact to remember is that "classification" of fingerprints and "identification" of fingerprints are two different and distinct concepts which have very little in common except that they both deal with fingerprints. The classification of a set of fingerprints is derived by a mathematical formula based on the types of patterns occurring on the ten fingers of an individual and the various sub-

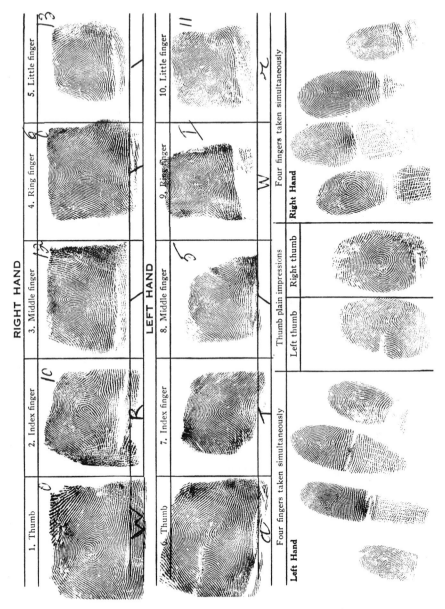

Figure 9. A fingerprint card with pattern symbols and ridge counting and tracing marked in the pattern blocks. The classification for this set of prints is

$$\frac{10 \quad 1 \quad R \quad 13}{18 \quad aT\text{--}r}$$

classifications and divisions given to these patterns upon the basis of the location, within the patterns, of fixed reference points such as deltas and cores.

Identification, on the other hand, is concerned with a comparison of individual ridge characteristics (rather than pattern types), such as bifurcations, ridge endings, enclosures and ridge dots. Figure 10 illustrates the most important types of ridge characteristics.

Before it can be said that two fingerprint impressions were produced by the same finger, the patterns must of course be of the same type. That, however, is largely insufficient and relatively meaningless, since all fingerprints can be brought within three gen-

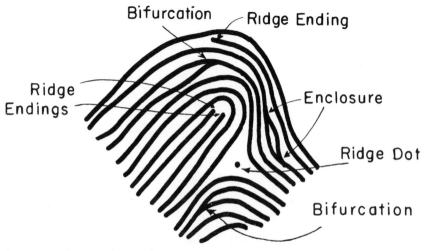

Figure 10. The most frequently encountered ridge characteristics are pointed out in this fingerprint drawing. Courtesy: Institute of Applied Science

eral classes of patterns. To establish identity, therefore, it must be shown that a sufficient number of ridge characteristics are found in the same position and in the same relative frequency (both quantitatively and qualitatively) in both finger impressions, and that no unexplainable differences exist.

FINGERPRINT CLASSIFICATION

Pattern Interpretation

The classification formula of a set of fingerprints is arrived at after going through a preliminary process known as pattern interpretation and blocking out. All fingerprints can be brought within one of three main pattern groups: arches, loops and whorls. Arches account for approximately 5% of all fingerprints; loops, approximately 60%; whorls, 35%.

Arches are subdivided into plain arches and tented arches. Loops are initially subdivided into ulnar and radial loops, depending upon the slant of the loop and the hand on which they appear; they are further subdivided by a process known as ridge counting. Whorl-type patterns are divided into four subgroups: plain whorls, central pocket loops, double loops and accidental whorls. They, too, may be further subdivided by a process known as ridge tracing. Figure 11 is a display of all of the pattern groups.

Technical rules exist to determine within which class of patterns a given fingerprint falls. These rules are studied by fingerprint technicians and then applied to the prints on a card, so that all fingerprint technicians will assign the same interpretation to a given pattern. Some patterns seem a little doubtful; they appear to fit into more than one category and different technicians might arrive at a different pattern interpretation. If this happens, the technician who is in doubt assigns to the print the symbol of the pattern which it most strongly appears to be, and then also assigns a secondary interpretation to it based on what he feels another equally qualified technician might call it. Patterns of that type are called questionable or approximating patterns. The technician will assign two classifications to the set of prints, one based on his original interpretation of the questioned pattern and one based on the alternative interpretation. This latter classification is known as a reference classification. In searching through a file, both classifications will be searched to ensure that an individual's identification will not be overlooked simply because one technician had a different idea about the type of pattern with which he was dealing.

Within all loop and whorl patterns there are also fixed reference points known as deltas. Loops have one delta each. Plain whorls, central pocket loops and double loops have two deltas, while accidental whorls have at least two deltas but can have more. The delta is formed by a ridge characteristic usually located near the lower edge of a print. Another fixed reference point in loops is the core. It is formed by a ridge characteristic near the center of the pattern. There are arbitrary rules, set up by the fingerprint pioneers who devised the classification schemes, which the technicians follow to de-

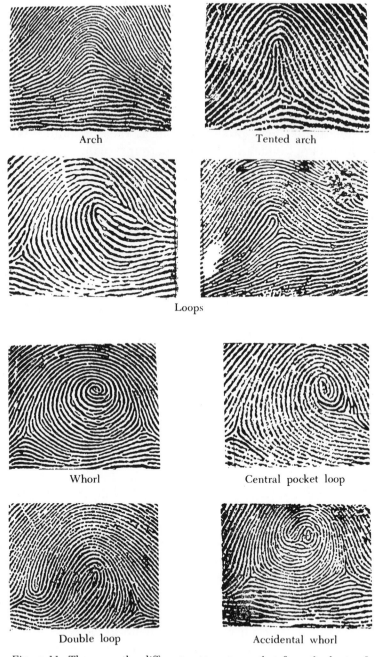

Arch

Tented arch

Loops

Whorl

Central pocket loop

Double loop

Accidental whorl

Figure 11. These are the different pattern types that form the basis of the classification system used in American identification services.

termine the exact location, within a pattern, of the core and delta.

Ridge counting in loops is a process of counting all the ridges that cross an imaginary line drawn between the core and the delta, not counting these two reference points themselves. Figure 12 illustrates this process. Ridge tracing in whorls is a process in which the line or friction skin detail that constitutes the left delta is traced toward the right delta. If the traced ridge flows above or to the inside

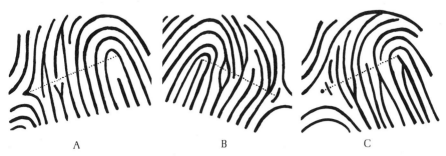

A   B   C

Figure 12. In these three fingerprint drawings, the dotted line illustrates the process of ridge counting in loops. Pattern A has a ridge count of seven, B a count of ten, and C a count of eight.

of the right delta by three or more ridges, the whorl is called inner (symbol I); if the traced ridge meets the right delta or passes either over or under it with not more than two intervening ridges, the whorl is called meeting (symbol M); if the ridge traced from the left delta flows under or to the outside of the right delta by three of more ridges, the pattern is called outer (symbol O). The process of ridge tracing is illustrated in Figure 13.

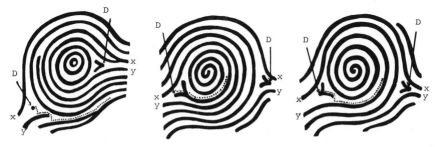

Figure 13. The three whorl patterns show the process of ridge tracing. The pattern on the far left is an outer whorl, the pattern in the center an inner whorl, and the one on the right a meeting whorl. The dotted line in the illustration shows how the tracing is done.

Blocking Out

The process of interpreting and blocking out a set of fingerprints is completed with the placing, upon the card, of the symbols of all of the patterns according to a definite procedure, as well as recording the ridge counts for loops and the ridge traces for whorls in the upper right-hand corner of all rolled print blocks. Looking back at Figure 9, the correct use of blocking-out symbols needed for that set may be observed on the fingerprint card.

Determining Classification

The classification of a set of fingerprints is a formula written in the form of a fraction with a numerator and a denominator. It is composed of a series of separate elements, the nature of which differs depending on the classification system in use by the agency. Initially, most American identification bureaus adopted the system developed by the Englishman Edward R. Henry in the late 1890s. This system worked quite satisfactorily for collections of up to 100,000 sets of prints. As files grew more voluminous, the Henry system was expanded step by step to make it workable for the larger accumulations of fingerprints in the metropolitan police agencies, state bureaus and the FBI. Collectively, these various "modifications and extensions to the Henry system," as they were originally known, have become known as the FBI system.

The basic components of a classification formula comprise a primary, secondary, subsecondary, major division, final and key. Within the formula, the symbols that represent these components are not written in the same order, although the filing and searching sequence follows the aforementioned order: primary, secondary, subsecondary, major, final and key. A typical classification formula, with its separate components identified, follows here:

| | | Pri- | Secon- | Sub- | |
Key	Major	mary	dary	secondary	Final
7	I	6	U	IOO	12
	O	16	Ur	OOM	

The FBI, and a few of the larger bureaus, use several additional extensions in those portions of the file where the full classification still does not afford a sufficient breakdown of the cards. These extensions are called the SML extension, the numerical extension and the WCDX extension. The process of determining the classification follows very definite rules, which are fully described in *Fingerprint Techniques*, by Andre A. Moenssens.

FINGERPRINT IDENTIFICATION

In comparing an unknown latent impression with an inked impression of known origin in order to determine whether or not both were made by the same finger, the technician looks for four different elements: the likeness of the general pattern type (or, if the type cannot be determined because the questioned pattern is incomplete, for a general similarity in the flow of the ridges); the qualitative likeness of the friction ridge characteristics; the quantitative likeness of the friction ridge characteristics; the likeness of location of the characteristics.

Many latent impressions found at crime scenes are badly blurred or smudged. Such prints cannot be used for the purpose of determining their origin. Some partially blurred prints, also quite frequently found, can be used to establish identity if the area of friction skin that is not blurred or obliterated is sufficiently large to contain not less than eight clearly distinguishable ridge characteristics. Most experts prefer to find at least 10 or 12 ridge concordances between the unknown and known prints.

In comparing latent prints with inked impressions, a number of apparent dissimilarities may be observed. If these differences are explainable as being caused by ordinary pressure distortion (very common), or by partial blurring or filling up of ridges with developing powder, or by superimpositions, they have no effect on the process of establishing identity. Should an unexplained dissimilarity occur, however, as for example the appearance of a clearly defined ridge characteristic in the latent print which does not appear in the inked impressions, then the conclusion is warranted that the prints were not made by the same finger.

In extensive testing and research with tens of thousands of "similar" though not identical prints, experts have been unable to find more than three characteristics that are quantitatively and qualitatively the same in two prints known to be from different fingers. By selecting a requirement of at least eight matching characteristics in both prints, a degree of certainty is introduced, and that accounts for the fact that there is very seldom a "battle of opposing experts" in fingerprint cases.

LATENT PRINT DEVELOPMENT

Whenever policemen are sent to a crime scene, their primary aims ought to be to preserve the evidence, prevent its contamination or destruction, and make it possible for the evidence technicians to gather the available trace evidence. Trace evidence is any type of physical evidence that might be discovered at a crime scene, including paper, matches, arms and ammunition, hairs, stains —in short, anything that could conceivably have bearing on or itself be evidence of a crime. In carrying out those three obligations, the policeman who first arrives at the scene should make an effort to remove all persons from the area to another place where they can be questioned, but in such a manner that nothing is touched at the crime scene. The officer himself must be careful not to leave his own fingerprints or destroy prints on door handles, windows, furniture and other objects or places. He should also be careful not to disturb the scene in any other way, such as by moving furniture. Departmental procedures will instruct him on what his other duties are and in which order they should be performed.

Ordinarily, an injured victim will first be examined by a doctor and then removed from the scene, even if this must result in some disturbance. When the victim is deceased, however, he or she is not ordinarily removed until after the police photographer has taken a complete series of photographs of the scene. The fingerprint technician is usually next to start his search for latent fingerprints, although other evidence technicians may start gathering trace evidence at the same time.

In order to develop latent impressions, the technician ordinarily uses specially prepared fingerprint powders. He can also use certain vapors (such as iodine fumes) or chemicals. Small objects that might contain fingerprints are first photographed in place, then carefully picked up, labeled and packed in special containers devised to protect any latent prints from accidental destruction or smudging, and transported to the police station or crime laboratory for fingerprint search. In the crime laboratory, the technician might use chemical solutions, such as silver nitrate or ninhydrin, to discover the presence of latent prints. Doors, heavy furniture and walls are usually "dusted" for fingerprints right at the crime scene. See Figure 14 for an illustration of developed crime scene latent prints.

When latent prints have been discovered and developed, and the technician determines that they are of such a quality that they might lead to an identification, the latent print is photographed on the object where it was discovered. If the object is easy to move, the developed latent print will be left in place and may be protected by a piece of cellophane. The object is then taken to the evidence room at the police station or crime laboratory so that it may later be used as evidence.

If the object is not portable, the developed latent print will be "lifted" from the place where it was found and transferred to a special latent print transfer card with appropriate notations as to exactly where it was found, under what conditions, by whom and at

Figure 14. Many latent fingerprints were visible on a portion of a bottle after it was treated with gray fingerprint powder.

what time. This process of lifting can be done by means of opaque rubber lifters, transparent cellophane lifts or special fingerprinting tape similar to ordinary Scotch tape.

Processing a crime scene for the presence of latent fingerprints requires special skills that are not ordinarily known to the investigating police officer. It is extremely important, therefore, that the investigators do not attempt to make a crime scene search for fingerprints unless they have had this special training.

Although the FBI will not conduct crime scene searches on behalf of a local law enforcement agency, its crime laboratory in Washington, D.C., is available for the scientific analysis and examination of items of evidence sent to it, including the examination of objects for the presence of latent fingerprints and the comparison of latent prints with recorded, inked impressions for the purpose of determining whether the latent prints can be identified. Items sent to the FBI must be carefully wrapped, boxed and shipped according to standard procedures and directives of the FBI. The FBI bulletins that refer to these processes are titled *An Outline of the Rules for Handling Physical Evidence* and *Suggestions for Handling Physical Evidence.* The latter consists of a detailed chart to be used in submitting evidence to the FBI laboratory. Both of these bulletins are reprinted in the appendix to this volume. Whenever expert services have been requested from the FBI, it will furnish a qualified laboratory examiner to testify to his conclusions and findings if his presence at a trial is needed.

At some point during the investigation of a crime it will become necessary to record the fingerprints of all persons who were present at the crime scene, including those of the investigating police officers and those of persons who were not present but who normally have legitimate access to the premises. These fingerprint cards will be needed by the technicians who process and compare latent fingerprints in order to eliminate latent traces and concentrate on establishing the identity of those prints which remain unidentified after the known prints are screened out.

When one or more unidentified latent prints are left over, they may be compared with the recorded prints of persons suspected of having committed the crime whose identity is known through eye witnesses or other investigative procedures. If these persons are fugitives, a search of the alphabetical name cards at the police department may reveal the existence of a set of recorded fingerprints. If that is the case, their fingerprint cards may be retrieved from the file so that they can be compared with the unknown latent prints.

It must be understood that if the identity of suspects is not known it is not possible to go to the main fingerprint file and search through it to establish the identity of latent prints. Fingerprint cards are filed according to a classification formula that is derived from a study of *all ten* of the fingers on a card. When only one or a few latent prints are found, it is impossible to make up a classification formula that will enable technicians to go to the main fingerprint file and search the appropriate section unless all or nearly all of the cards can be checked individually—an obviously impossible task, considering that fingerprint cards number in the millions in even medium-sized identification bureaus. It is therefore necessary either to have a suspect physically present so that his fingerprints can be recorded for comparison or to know the name of a suspect so that his fingerprint classification, and ultimately his fingerprint card, can be discovered in the main file.

To overcome this great handicap, many departments maintain special fingerprint collections of habitual criminals of the type that are likely to leave latent fingerprints at crime scenes, such as burglars, auto thieves and the like. These collections, which are much smaller than the main fingerprint files, are maintained on the basis of different classification systems that make them more useful for latent print searches. Some of these files contain individual fingerprints rather than ten-finger cards; others are so-called five-finger systems in which two cards per individual, one for each hand, are filed separately, thus cutting down on the number of possible reference searches.

Research has been going on for years to do away with the conventional classification and filing system and to replace it with a totally automated, computer-controlled optical scanning system. Tremendous progress has been made in that direction. Computers are already being used to speed up much of the fingerprint retrieval work, but a totally automated system is not yet a reality. It may be expected, however, that a revolutionary method will be in operation within the next decade or two.

FINGERPRINT EVIDENCE IN COURT

Fingerprint evidence linking a defendant to a crime scene has been widely and uniformly admitted in American courts. Experts whose qualifications have been established to the satisfaction of the

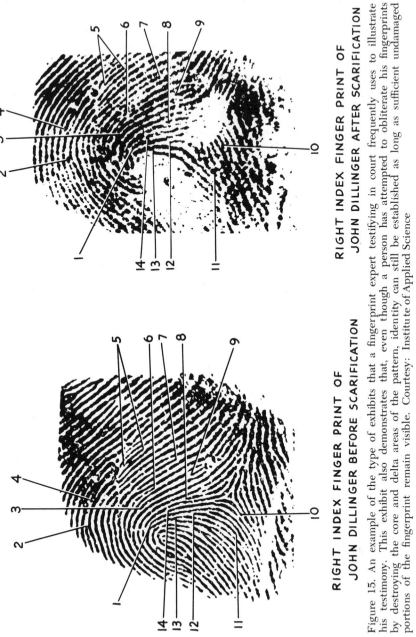

RIGHT INDEX FINGER PRINT OF
JOHN DILLINGER BEFORE SCARIFICATION

RIGHT INDEX FINGER PRINT OF
JOHN DILLINGER AFTER SCARIFICATION

Figure 15. An example of the type of exhibits that a fingerprint expert testifying in court frequently uses to illustrate his testimony. This exhibit also demonstrates that, even though a person has attempted to obliterate his fingerprints by destroying the core and delta areas of the pattern, identity can still be established as long as sufficient undamaged portions of the fingerprint remain visible. Courtesy: Institute of Applied Science

judge are permitted to give their opinions in court as to whether or not the fingerprints found at the scene of a crime correspond to those of a particular defendant. Courts have accepted as true, without further proof of reliability, that fingerprints offer a reliable means of positively identifying individuals.

Fingerprints cannot be used as evidence against a defendant if they are discovered in areas to which the defendant might have had innocent access, as in the public areas of stores, bars, gasoline stations and the like, unless it can be positively established that the fingerprints were left at the time of the commission of the crime.

When an expert presents his evidence before a court, he often uses enlarged photographs of both the latent print and the known, inked print. An exhibit of such a type is illustrated in Figure 15. The expert draws lines pointing to specific ridge characteristics in both the latent and the inked prints. By assigning the same number to a given characteristic appearing in both prints, he can explain to the court and jury how he reached his conclusion of identity. The book *Fingerprints and the Law* presents a detailed discussion of how fingerprint evidence is introduced at a trial and how an expert might go about persuading fact finders of the correctness of his conclusions.

Recorded, inked fingerprints that are used in court for comparison with latent crime scene prints are also freely admissible in court, provided the prints have been recorded following a lawful arrest or in accordance with state statutes dealing with the right to take fingerprints.

REFERENCES

Bridges, *Practical Fingerprinting*, 2nd ed., Funk & Wagnalls Company (New York), 1963.

Cummins and Midlo, *Finger Prints, Palms and Soles*, 2nd ed., Dover Publications (New York), 1964.

Federal Bureau of Investigation, *The Science of Fingerprints*, United States Government Printing Office (Washington, D.C.), 1963.

Moenssens, *Fingerprints and the Law*, Chilton Book Company (Philadelphia), 1969.

Moenssens, *Fingerprint Techniques*, Chilton Book Company (Philadelphia), 1971.

Chapter 3

Questioned Documents

The determination of the genuineness of handwriting, and of documents generally, has been an issue in litigation for centuries. The scientific examination of questioned documents, however, did not develop into a profession until about 1870, even though prior to that time certain legal photographers had made an attempt to reveal forged writings by the use of photography. During the 1860s some photographers pretended to be document examiners: photographic enlargements gave them a previously unknown means of studying and visually displaying minute portions of handwritings and signatures.

The Frenchman, Alphonse Bertillon, whom we mentioned in the preceding chapter as the developer of anthropometry, was also a master photographer who fancied himself as a great document expert. He frequently gave opinions on the genuineness of documents, and these opinions, coming as they did from the head of the French identification service, carried great weight. It was Bertillon the photographer and anthropometrist who provided some of the damning evidence in the famous Dreyfus affair (which resulted in Emile Zola's famous manifesto, *J'accuse*) by testifying that Alfred Dreyfus had written the document which served as the basis for his conviction for treason and subsequent banishment. Later, of course, Dreyfus' innocence was established, as well as Bertillon's error in testifying that Dreyfus wrote the incriminating document. Bertillon's mistaken opinion was the result of his lack of expertise in the comparison of handwritings. The incident demonstrates probably more dramatically than any other example that a photographer is not a person qualified to give opinions on the identity of handwritings—

not even a photographer who is experienced in making minute and accurate measurements of apparently insignificant trace evidence, as Bertillon was.

Over the years, the examination of questioned documents developed into a profession all its own, and it came to be recognized that special skills and training were required before a person could achieve the competence to give opinions on the genuineness of documents. It was also recognized that, while photographers were not by virtue of their profession also handwriting experts, photography was a useful tool for questioned document examiners. As scientific progress made its influence felt in all human endeavors, so did men working with documents begin to apply sophisticated techniques in their job.

Today, the competent questioned document examiner has knowledge of and uses various sciences, including chemistry and microscopy as well as photography, in determining the genuineness of a document. A distinction should be made between the professional document examiner and graphologists or persons practicing any systems of handwriting study based on graphology, such as handwriting analysts, graphoanalysts or grapho-readers. The latter purport to assess personality and character upon a study of an individual's handwriting, an art that has its prominent advocates as well as critics who question its validity. Graphology is taught as part of the required curriculum for psychologists at a number of European universities although it has not been formally adopted by American institutions of higher learning. Graphology, under whatever system it may be taught, is quite different from questioned document examination, which is concerned with establishing the genuineness, or lack of it, of disputed documents on the basis of comparison with known standards. Graphologists, therefore, lack the qualifications and training required for professional document examinations of the type needed in criminal investigation and the establishment of courtroom proof, unless they have acquired training and experience in document work quite separate and distinct from their graphological studies.

Questioned Documents and Standards of Comparison

In questioned document work, a document is "questioned" when any doubt arises about the authenticity of it or any of its parts. The doubt may center around the authorship of a letter but could just as well be concerned with whether a minute change has been made on an otherwise genuine document, such as the erasure of a name or dollar amount on a check and the substitution of a different name and a higher, or lower, amount.

"Document" means any type of paper, cardboard or material on which there may appear any signature, handwriting, handprinting, typewriting, printing or other graphic marks, the authenticity of which is in dispute or doubtful. Although the questioned document examiner is involved mostly in the study of papers, the use of the word "document" may at times be misleading when a message is conveyed on a material other than paper. The study of questioned documents involves messages of all kinds contained in letters, but it also includes such items as checks, telephone messages, telegrams, ledger entries, hotel or motel registration slips, drivers' licenses, wills, birth certificates, passports, application forms, examination books or papers, diplomas, lottery or gambling slips, shipping or Addressograph labels and even newspapers. In addition, the examiner of documents may well be called in to study writing, printing or other marks made on boxes, the walls of washrooms, the wood of doors or even the walls of buildings in the street.

The job of the document examiner is not limited to determining whether some handwriting or typewriting has been made by a suspected individual. He is also concerned with other facets of forgery detection. Among them are the authentication and dating of documents; the decipherment of erased, obliterated, charred and water-damaged documents; the restoration of faded and chemically erased writings. Related problems he deals with involve the sequencing of a great number of writings or documents; a study of additions, interlineations and interpolations; rubber stamp and seal impressions; fluid ink and ball-point pen ink analysis; pencil marks; indented writings; suspected substitution of pages; the study of paper watermarks and of printing, copying and duplication processes; and the detection of alterations.

Competent questioned document examiners own or work with quite elaborate laboratories equipped with stereoscopic microscopes and other general and specialized optical instruments; various types of light sources or illumination, including "invisible" light techniques previously discussed in the chapter on photography; and expensive calibrating and measuring apparatuses. The laboratory must include complete photographic facilities for the reproduction of documents, using the most up-to-date techniques, as well as equipment for the production and mounting of court exhibits and other modern visual aids for court use. An extensive reference library usually complements the laboratory facilities.

Since documents are handled by individuals, it may also be important to determine the presence of fingerprints. That job is usually not within the expertise of the document examiner, and he will have to cooperate with a fingerprint technician. This imposes upon both the questioned document examiner and the fingerprint technician a duty to conduct their examinations of the same document in such a manner as not to interfere with, or make impossible, the other's work.

A questioned document should be handled as little as possible and with the utmost care. In any handling that is necessary, tweezers should be used or else fingers should touch only the tips of the paper. The writer's fingerprints, if present thereon, might otherwise be destroyed, or decipherable indentations or other marks of value to the document examiner may be damaged. Under no circumstances should a pencil or pen be used to point out to another person the characteristics on a document.

To transport a questioned document, the investigator should use an envelope, preferably plastic, that is big enough that no folding of the document will be required.

Handwriting Standards

When the issue is one of establishing the identity of the writer of a document, or the genuineness of it, the examiner needs to compare it with other documents of known origin. Such documents are called "standards." Before a writing can be used as a standard for comparison, its origin must be positively established. This origin may be established by having the suspect give a sample of his writing in the presence of an examiner or by having him acknowledge his authorship of older letters and documents. The origin may also be established by the testimony of witnesses who saw a writing executed or by persons familiar with the writing, or the very nature of the specimen may serve to authenticate it as a standard. For instance, the writing on an employment application or in a letter responding to someone's communication would constitute self-authenticating documents. Preexisting standards should have been made as near as possible to the date on which the questioned writing was supposed to have been executed. When obtaining a request writing, it is usually a good practice to have the subject write down the text of the disputed document while it is being dictated to him. Supplementary request writings may be obtained by dictating different copy to the suspect.

After a number of years of experimentation the Chicago Police Scientific Crime Detection Laboratory (now officially called the Criminalistics Division) adopted the practice of having a suspected writer fill out the form reproduced here as Figure 16A and B. Its principal designer, document examiner David J. Purtell, has found that the specimens thereby obtained are adequate for practically every type of criminal case. (A police department that contemplates using a similar form should consult Captain Purtell's article in 54 *Journal of Criminal Law, Criminology and Police Science* 522 [1963], in which he recommends using colored ink, preferably light blue, for the inner lines on the form so that they can be filtered out photographically later on for purposes of courtroom handwriting comparison.)

In check forgery cases, Captain Purtell recommends using as a standard a check form printed on "safety" paper similar to that used for regular checks but with the word "STANDARD" appearing in the place where a bank name normally appears. Such a practice should allay the fears of anyone who may think he is being tricked into committing a real check forgery.

Standards may be obtained from a variety of sources other than request writings. One document examiner, Donald Doud, has suggested the following as possible sources of standard writings, including signatures:

	General		Applications for
1.	Letters, personal and business	26.	Light
		27.	Power
2.	Postcards	28.	Water
3.	Manuscripts	29.	Gas
4.	Memoranda	30.	Steam
5.	Occupational writings	31.	Telephone
6.	Checks	32.	Credit accounts
7.	Endorsements on checks	33.	Positions

NAME	DATE	
ADDRESS	CITY & STATE	PHONE
MARRIED OR SINGLE	NAME OF SPOUSE	
CITY & STATE OF BIRTH	DATE OF BIRTH	
NAME OF PERSON LIVING WITH	RELATIONSHIP	
OCCUPATION (IF STUDENT LIST SCHOOL)	SOCIAL SECURITY NUMBER	
NAME OF EMPLOYER OR FORMER EMPLOYER	SALARY	
ADDRESS OF EMPLOYER	PHONE	
NAME OF NEAREST RELATIVE	RELATIONSHIP	
ADDRESS OF NEAREST RELATIVE	CITY & STATE	

WRITE THE FOLLOWING	WRITE THE FOLLOWING
ALBERT JOHNSON	DONALD O'CONNOR
EDWARD YOUNGBERG	ROBERT OLSEN
MICHAEL SMITH	PETER FISHER
CHARLES QUINN	JACK KOWALSKI
GEORGE KELLY	U. X. ZIMMERMAN
DAVIES McINTYRE	ELIZABETH VAUGHN
WILLIAM BROWN	FRANKLIN PATRICK
RAYMOND TAYLOR	LAWRENCE HARRISON
THOMAS NOVAK	YOUR SIGNATURE

LAB NO. ______

NAME ______

CHICAGO POLICE DEPARTMENT
CRIME LABORATORY

NAT ______
S ______
B ______
H ______
W ______

R A C S C D N A N S H D R L Y M S L

Figure 16A.

WRITE THE FOLLOWING

NAME	DATE
6739 N. FOURTH AVE.	LAKE PARKER, WASHINGTON
4258 S. INDIANA BLVD.	MANCHESTER CITY, VIRGINIA
6125 W. KILPATRICK RD.	BLACK WOODS, NEW JERSEY
8039 E. 47TH ST.	ANDERSON HILL, GEORGIA

FIFTY SEVEN DOLLARS AND THIRTY TWO CENTS	$ 57.32	JUNE 24, 1967 19____
ONE HUNDRED EIGHTY NINE DOLLARS & NO CENTS	$ 189.00	DEC. 30, 1958 19____

HANDPRINT THE FOLLOWING MESSAGE ABOVE THE WORDS SHOWN

T H E   M O N E Y   I N   D O L L A R S   W H I C H   D I C K   Z A S S   R E C E I V E D   F R O M   V I R G I N I A

M C L O N G   W A S   P L A C E D   I N   H E R   A U T O   W I T H O U T   A N Y   T R O U B L E.   I T   W A S   L A Y I N G

C O V E R E D   B Y   A   S L I C K   C A P E   A N D   W I T H   L U C K   W O U L D   N E V E R   B E   F O U N D

B U T   A   P U S S Y   J U M P E D   O N   T H E   S E A T   A N D   K I L L E D   T H E   O B N O X I O U S   T R I C K.

USE THIS SPACE FOR DICTATED MATERIAL

SIGNATURE	WITNESSED BY

CPD–24.639 (REV.11/62)

INSTRUCTIONS TO INVESTIGATOR IN OBTAINING REPRESENTATIVE WRITING SPECIMENS: 1. To complete this form, sit the writer at a desk provided with a normal nib fountain pen. Instruct him to answer every question in handwriting or handprinting using no abbreviations. 2. ADDITIONAL STANDARDS should be obtained by duplicating the original paper and writing instrument and dictating, at least 3 times, selected portions of the questioned document without aiding in spelling or punctuation. In check cases use voided checks. 3. Also obtain driver's license, identification cards, applications, personal letters, etc. 4. Officer obtaining standards will see that every line is completed and then sign as witness.

Figure 16B.

General (*continued*)   Applications for (*continued*)

8. Withdrawal slips   34. Memberships
   (savings accounts)   35. Insurance
9. Bank deposit slips   36. Gasoline, tires,
10. Bank signature cards   autos, etc.
11. Drafts   (government)
12. Deeds   37. Passports
13. Contracts   38. Surety bonds
14. Notes   39. Bank and trust company
15. Complaints (legal)   loans
16. Administrators' reports 40. Marriage licenses
17. Agreements   41. Dog licenses
18. Wills   42. Business licenses
19. Mortgages
20. Affidavits
21. Bills of sale
22. Partnership agreements
23. Petitions
24. Leases
25. Transcribed (signed)
    testimony

It should be obvious by now that the matter of first importance in obtaining a standard is to examine the questioned writing in order to be able to choose a form that most closely resembles that of the questioned writing and then to decide on a manner of execution that most closely resembles the conditions under which the questioned document was written. For instance, if the questioned one was made on unruled paper, the dictated standard should be made on unruled paper of the same color, thickness and quality. For similar reasons, the writer of the standard should be supplied with the same type of writing instrument that was used for the questioned document. The same general kind of writing should be requested, too (for instance, if the questioned document was handprinted, handprinting should be requested). Under no circumstances should the writer be told how to spell any word, even if he asks.

Typewriting Standards

When the origin, identity or genuineness of a typewritten document is at issue and it becomes necessary to establish whether or not it has been typed on a particular typewriter, the only standards would be samples of the type produced by the suspected typewriter. These samples would be compared with the questioned typescript. It is important that the standard contain all of the machine's characters and several copies of the questioned typing. A good format for obtaining typewriting standards is that utilized by the Criminalistics Division of the Chicago Police Department, which is illustrated in Figure 16C.

When a writing pad or a stack of typing paper is available as a preexisting standard, the whole pad or stack should be handed over to the document examiner, not just a few sheets of it. The more standards the examiner has to work with, the more likely it becomes that he will be able to reach a conclusion on the basis of his various comparisons.

HANDWRITING COMPARISONS

The comparison of handwriting is placed among the topics of scientific evidence because the document examiner uses many scientific principles and technological processes to aid him in his investigation, examination and evaluation. The theory upon which the document expert proceeds is that every time a person writes he automatically and subconsciously stamps his individuality in his writing. Through a careful analysis and interpretation of the individual and class characteristics, it is usually possible to determine whether the questioned document and the standards were written by the same person.

A great number of factors are considered when examining handwritten materials, although a forger usually acts on the false assumption that writings differ only in the design of the letters. A specimen of handwriting may have from 500 to 1,000 individual characteristics. Individuality is determined by considering such factors as form, movement, muscular habits, skill, instrument use, pen position, line quality, shading, retraces, proportions, connections, spacings, terminals, slant, alignment, punctuation and embellishments.

Figure 17 presents a good illustration of what the document examiner looks for when he compares two specimens of writing. Each of the fifteen specimens of "and," written by fifteen different writers, contains individual characteristics—characteristics which differ

FORMAT FOR TYPEWRITING STANDARDS

TYPEWRITER
IDENTIFICATION

IBM Electric Typewriter, Serial Number 11-95342, located
at 1111 South Michigan, 5th floor, Room 599, owned by
the Neverready Company and assigned to Mr. J. Jones.

ENTIRE
KEYBOARD
--TWICE

```
ABCDEFGHIJKLMNOPQRSTUVWXYZ          ABCDEFGHIJKLMNOPQRSTUVWXYZ
abcdefghijklmnopqrstuvwxyz          abcdefghijklmnopqrstuvwxyz
1234567890-=½;',./                  1234567890-=½;',./
!@#$%¢&*()_+¼:",.?                  !@#$%¢&*()_+¼:",.?
```

MESSAGE

This is a warning to you and your family. We know where

you live. If you don't put $10,000 in a brown envelope

and place it under the rock near the second pillar North

of the "L" station on Ashland Ave. we will kill your son.

We mean business.

This is a warning to you and your family. We know where

you live. If you don't put $10,000 in a brown envelope

and place it under the rock near the second pillar North

of the "L" station on Ashland Ave. we will kill your son.

We mean business.

CARBON PAPER
IMPRESSION

ENTIRE
KEYBOARD

```
ABCDEFGHIJKLMNOPQRSTUVWXYZ          ABCDEFGHIJKLMNOPQRSTUVWXYZ
abcdefghijklmnopqrstuvwxyz          abcdefghijklmnopqrstuvwxyz
1234567890-=½;',./                  1234567890-=½;',./
!@#$%¢&*()_+¼:",.?                  !@#$%¢&*()_+¼:",.?
```

MESSAGE

This is a warning to you and your family. We know where

you live. If you don't put $10,000 in a brown envelope

and place it under the rock near the second pillar North

of the "L" station on Ashland Ave. we will kill your son.

We mean business.

TYPIST
IDENTIFICATION

This material was typed by Det. Earl E. Morn, #1961,
45th Dist., on 31 January 1971 at the above listed location.

TO OBTAIN CARBON PAPER IMPRESSION--SET MACHINE FOR STENCIL AND PLACE
CARBON PAPER IN FRONT OF TYPING PAPER

WHEN TYPING, VARY DEGREE OF TOUCH--HEAVY, MEDIUM AND LIGHT

Figure 16C.

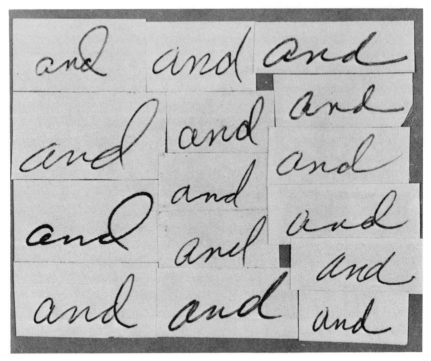

Figure 17. The word "and" as written by fifteen different persons. A comparison of any one "and" with the other fourteen will reveal not only differences in the total formation of the word but also differences in the individual letters composing it. Note, for instance, the various ways in which the "a" is started.

from those found in the writings of other individuals. Subsequent illustrations serve to demonstrate how the comparisons are made and the manner in which the evidence is presented in court.

One of the most noteworthy document cases ever to be brought before an American jury involved the kidnapping and subsequent killing of the infant child of the famous aviator Charles Lindbergh in 1932. The prosecution rested its case against Bruno Hauptmann primarily upon the testimony of handwriting experts who determined that the fifteen ransom notes sent to the Lindbergh family came from Hauptmann's hand.

The eight document examiners in the Hauptmann case were unanimous in the opinion that Hauptmann had written the fifteen ransom letters, the addresses on the envelopes in which they had been mailed, and the address on the wrapper of the package containing the sleeping suit of the baby which the kidnapper had sent to Lindbergh to prove that he was dealing with the person who had the child.

The conclusion of one of the experts, Clark Sellers of Los Angeles, was based on a great number of factors. He illustrated his findings by referring to some of the details visible in selected words and numerals. One of these exhibits, shown in Figure 18, which incidentally also illustrates the type of demonstrative evidence generally used by questioned document examiners in court, relates to the manner and varied forms in which the word "the" was written. One of the unique forms in these documents, according to Sellers, is the writing of the word "the" so that it appears (in A) to be "Ue." There is no hump on the "h." Still another form (in C) is in making the "t" with an upstroke and crossing it at the bottom, giving it the appearance of being a capital letter "S." A rare variation on the word "the" (in D) occurred in the oddity of transposing the "h" and the "t" so

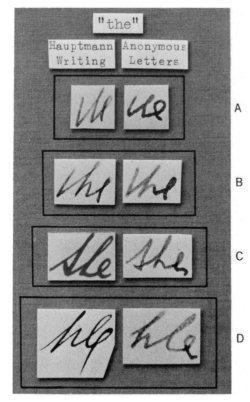

Figure 18. Courtesy: Clark Sellers

that the word appears to be "hle." This varied combination of form in the writing of the word "the" was of great identification value. Such a combination of variations makes it difficult, if not impossible, for a writer to successfully imitate the writing of another, and practically precludes the possibility of two writers accidentally adopting the same form.

Numerals in a questioned document also have great identification value. In the court exhibit illustrated as Figure 19, Sellers showed that Hauptmann had developed certain divergencies from the copybook style of writing numerals.

The ransom notes did not contain a signature, but Sellers concluded that Hauptmann might just as well have signed his name to the anonymous letters. He displayed Hauptmann's signature as written on one of the known standards (see Figure 20) and pieced together Hauptmann's name with letters cut out of the anonymous letters. The "signature" thus reconstructed shows a surprising similarity to the known signature of Bruno Hauptmann.

Dissimilarities in handwriting specimens are just as important as similarities since they may tend to prove that the questioned writing was *not* written by the same individual who furnished the exemplar. Dissimilarities in the formation of capital letters are usually less indicative of nonidentity than dissimilarities in small letters. Capital letters occur less frequently and the forger or anonymous writer usually pays particular attention to totally changing the appearance of capital letters. He attempts to do the same with small letters, of course, but because there are many more of them, and because they are less given to variation, he is less successful in disguising his handwriting or imitating someone else's.

An excellent illustration of the details a document examiner looks for in determining whether a questioned signature is genuine or forged appears in Figure 21. Before you read how an examiner would eliminate forgeries, though, try a little experiment. Without reading beyond this paragraph, compare each one of the signatures on the left (the "questioned" specimens) with the genuine ones (the "standards") on the right. Seek to determine which, if any, of the questioned signatures on the left were written by the person who wrote the six signatures on the right.

Now compare your findings with the correct evaluation. A is a freehand writing of the name "Harold C. Havighurst" without any attempt to imitate the genuine signature. It is generally similar to

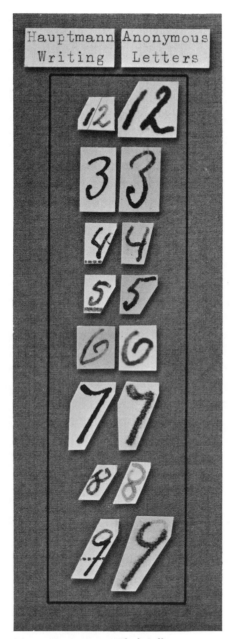

Figure 19. Courtesy: Clark Sellers

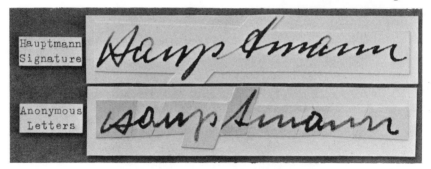

Figure 20. Courtesy: Clark Sellers

the standards on the right but only in its "class characteristics," the result of both writers using the same general style of penmanship (for example, the "H," the C" and the "t"). But the signature lacks the "individual characteristics" of the genuine specimens.

B is a freehand forgery that was made by a person who possessed a high degree of skill at studying a signature and being able to imitate it closely with a free-moving pen. Nevertheless, to the examiner it is clearly a forgery. Note the heavy crossbars on the horizontal part of the "H" and the crossbar of the "t," in contrast to what appears in the genuine specimens. Other differences include the start of the "a" in "Harold" from a horizontal position in B, in con-

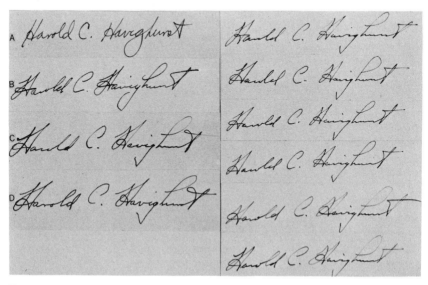

Figure 21.

trast to the angular start of the "a" in the standards; the angular connection between the "l" and the "d" in B, in contrast to the rounded form in the standards; and the longer lines connecting the "o" and "l" and the "v" and "i" in B, in contrast to the similar connections in the standards.

C is a genuine signature. It has many of the individual characteristics of the six standard specimens. There is a slight looping at the start of the crossbar of the "t," but this is consistent with the genuine writings at the right, which reveal a tendency toward such a loop formation.

D is an easy forgery for the expert to spot. It is a traced forgery —one made by placing a strong light under a glass, on which is placed a genuine signature that is traced onto the overlaying document being forged. By this process the forger makes a good imitation of the letter formations but because of his concentration on that effort he occasionally has to slow down the tracing, as is evident at the top of the "l" and in the downstroke of the "C." At times, he also has to lift the pen in order to keep on the track, and the evidence of this appears in the top loop of the "t."

THE DECIPHERMENT OF INDENTED WRITING, CHARRED DOCUMENTS AND EVIDENCE OF ALTERATIONS

Photography, ultraviolet light and occasionally infrared rays are valuable aids to the document examiner in handling such matters as indented writing, charred documents and suspected documentary alterations. When something is written on a piece of paper underneath which there are other papers, the underlying sheet may contain indentations that, if deciphered, may reveal what was on the top sheet. Such decipherments can be of inestimable value to the police investigator. For instance, a person who writes down a telephone number or other notation on a telephone pad may leave indented writing on an underlying sheet. That information, if deciphered, could lead to the identity of a criminal or to other evidence permitting the solution of a crime. Even what represents an original document, such as an extortion note, may have indentations on it of investigative or evidentiary value. The standard technique a document examiner uses in such cases is to photograph the piece of paper under oblique light so as to take advantage of the shadowing effect, which will frequently permit decipherment (see Figures 22A, B and C).

Photography can be used in many instances to decipher the writing on a document that has been charred in a fire, as shown in Figure 23. Charred documents must be handled with the utmost care by investigators; because of the fragility of charred documentary remains, the best procedure to follow is to refrain from disturbing them at all and leave the entire matter up to the document examiner.

Whenever suspicion arises about writing having been obliterated by the use of ink eradicators, the document may be subjected to ultraviolet light and the disclosure photographed, as shown in Figure 24. In that case, the original ink writing above a genuine signature had been removed with an ink eradicator and a different,

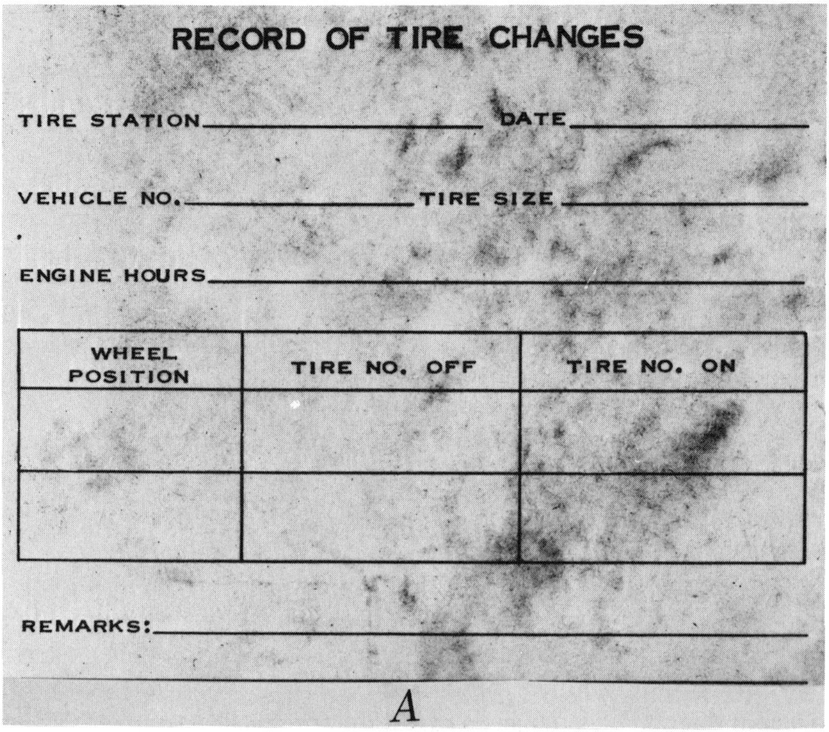

RECORD OF TIRE CHANGES

TIRE STATION_____ DATE_____

VEHICLE NO._____ TIRE SIZE_____

ENGINE HOURS_____

WHEEL POSITION	TIRE NO. OFF	TIRE NO. ON

REMARKS:_____

A

Figure 22. A is a document photographed in ordinary light. B is a photograph of the same document under oblique light. C was photographed with oblique light and a "Ronchi ruling plate," which served to diffuse the light and render the indentations more discernible.

B

typewritten message inserted in its place. Observe how ultraviolet light revealed the original writing and consequently disclosed the fraudulent nature of the typewritten instruction.

Infrared light may also be used to reveal suspected forgeries, as shown in Figure 25. In this illustration, A is a genuine signature and B is the questioned one. C is an infrared photograph of B and discloses an underlying pencil (carbon) tracing of the signature over which the inked copy was made. A tip-off that B may have been a traced forgery appears in the uneven flow of the writing, particularly in the "Jr." at the end.

SPECIAL CONSIDERATIONS IN HANDWRITING COMPARISONS

While the multitude of factors alluded to earlier are extremely important in studying questioned documents, the examiner cannot neglect to consider the influence of additional environmental fac-

C

tors which may have played a role in the production of the questioned samples. One such factor is opposite-hand writing.

The normally right-handed person might write an anonymous letter with his left hand, and vice versa. Normally, it is quite easy for the document examiner to spot writing with an unaccustomed hand, because the lack of muscular control is usually quite evident.

Even when the opposite hand has been used in an attempt to disguise one's writing, the writer will very likely display his individual writing characteristics to such a degree as to permit an identification. In all such instances, of course, it is highly desirable to obtain from such a suspect specimens of his opposite-hand writing.

Another consideration requires taking into account the writer's health at the time a writing is produced. This is especially true when it is necessary to determine if a writing that was allegedly written by an individual when he was in ill health or dying—as in the case of a will—was genuine rather than written by another interested party. Writings executed when one is of advanced age or in ill health or intoxicated are often so erratic and poorly written as

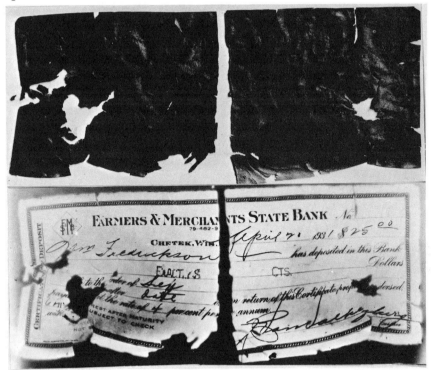

Figure 23. Charred document decipherment. The upper portion of the illustration shows the condition of a document burned in a fire. The lower photograph illustrates its decipherment by a special photographic process. Courtesy: John F. Tyrnell and Donald Doud.

to make them look like forgeries when in fact they are genuine. Problems of this kind tax the skill and experience of the examiner. He may at times be required to qualify his opinion, though in other instances he can arrive at a precise and definite conclusion. A crucial factor in deciding the issue is the availability of standards of comparison which are written when the person is in the same condition. If such standards are available, identification is likely not to present particular problems. Most frequently, however, the only available standards of writing are those that the purported writer executed at a much earlier time, when his health was good and his writing ability unimpaired. It is here that the task of the document expert becomes exceedingly difficult, and at times he may be unable to arrive at a definite conclusion.

The effect of age on handwriting can manifest itself in other ways as well. While it is not unusual for the writing of an individual to

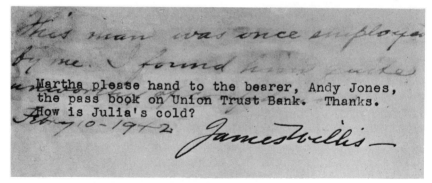

Martha please hand to the bearer, Andy Jones, the pass book on Union Trust Bank. Thanks. How is Julia's cold?

Figure 24. Decipherment of a forgery by ultraviolet photography. Courtesy: Ordway Hilton, Document Examiner, New York City

remain nearly identical throughout his whole life, there are a great number of individuals whose writing abilities and customs change throughout the years. This sometimes happens simply because a person changes to a job where he must write quickly. In developing speed, he sacrifices form, and his handwritings executed several

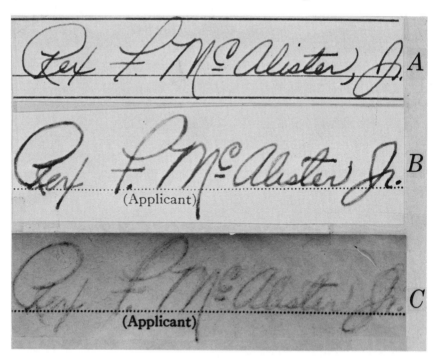

Figure 25.

years apart may look quite different. Other persons are more fastidious and constantly work at perfecting the writing style they use. Some have adopted the habit of writing their signatures in one way and then suddenly, at one point in their life, decide to adopt a totally different form of signature. The appearance of a writing may also vary according to the position of the writer (sitting, standing or leaning), the writing instrument used (pencil, fountain pen, ballpoint pen), the writer's mood (excited or depressed) and other factors. In obtaining standards, therefore, it is important to attempt to secure exemplars executed as close as possible in time to the date of the questioned writing and written under as similar circumstances as practicable.

If sufficient comparison data are available, many of these extraneous conditions may be minimized. However, when the questioned sample is meager in content, such as a single questioned signature appearing as an endorsement on a check, identification becomes much more difficult, and equally competent experts have been known to differ in their conclusions, or at least in the degree of certainty which they ascribe to their findings.

TYPEWRITING COMPARISONS

As with firearms identification, an appreciation of typewriter identification calls for some understanding of the processes involved in the manufacture of typewriters. The letters on a typewriter's keyboard are placed on type "slugs" by pressing soft metal into a matrix or die containing the standard type design for a particular machine. Initially, the type matrix is machine-engraved from a large drawing made by the typeface designer, and, as with automobiles and other manufactured products, each typewriter manufacturer has his own ideas about styles and shapes. Consequently, each manufacturer's products differ from the others. Moreover, each company may change its product from time to time (turn out new models). This is what makes it possible for a document examiner to ascertain, from a typewritten specimen, the make and model of the typewriter that produced the specimen (see Figure 26). In order to be able to determine make and model, the examiner must have at his disposal a reference collection of thousands of known type samples, and he must continue to keep his collection current by adding

Figure 26. Specimens of letters typed on four different makes of typewriters. Note the differences in the manufacturers' conceptions of what the letters should look like. Courtesy: Donald Doud

the typeface samples of newly introduced machines as they become available.

Once the make of the typewriter that produced a disputed type sample has been determined, it is possible to identify the specific machine by studying the individual characteristics peculiar to that machine. Typewriters develop individual characteristics through the wear of certain parts, the bending of type bars, the chipping of small fragments from the typeface characters, and so forth.

The collective factors that contribute to the individuality of a particular typewriter may be stated as follows: the vertical and horizontal alignment of characters in relation to each other; the vertical alignment of characters with respect to the horizontal base line of the writing; the variance of impression from top to bottom of particular type impressions resulting from maladjustment of the plane of the typeface and that of the paper surface; the condition of each typeface with respect to defects or damage; the relative weight on impression of a character as compared to other characters on the key board. For an example of typewriter identification by individual characteristics, see Figure 27.

We have been referring, up to now, to ordinary shift key typewriters. In 1961, a new type of machine was introduced by IBM which does not use typebars, namely the "Selectric" typewriter. In this type of machine, the writing is produced by a "type head" consisting of a ball of nickel-plated plastic bearing eleven rows of typeface, each row having four different faces. Unlike ordinary typewriters, the carriage of such machines does not move from right to left in the course of typing; instead, the carriage remains stationary and the type head moves, whirling to strike the ribbon and impress the characters on the paper, as with the common shift key machines. This model also develops individual characteristics which make it possible to identify the specific typewriters used to produce a questioned typing. Among these defects are vertical misalignment caused by a defective tilt mechanism, horizontal misalignment caused by a defective centering mechanism, uneven impressions caused by a head or roller that is out of alignment, and improper line spacing. One important feature about Selectric typewriters is that the type heads are also interchangeable from one machine to the next.

In recent years a number of anonymous letters have turned up which were written on "toy" typewriters. Identification data on toy typewriters was scarce for quite a long time. Recently, though, document examiners have accumulated much data on the subject, including information on type sizes and styles, inconsistency caused by crude mechanical parts, and the effect of various kinds of defective rollers on the quality of impression.

The analysis of printed matter for the purpose of differentiating between originals and reproductions, or to establish the source of a printed document, is also within the document examiner's competence. This presupposes knowledge of and familiarity with the printing process, movable type and Linotype systems of typesetting,

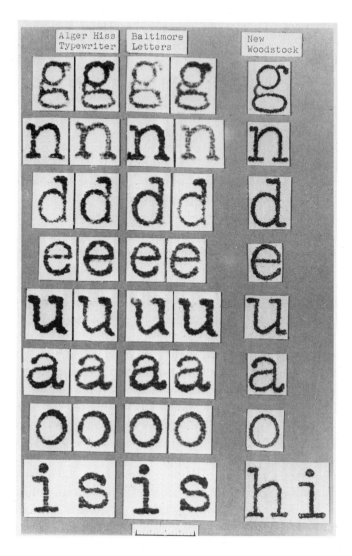

Figure 27. An illustration of how typewriter defects which are the results of wear and tear, may serve to identify a typewriter as being the one used to type a questioned document.

Alger Hiss, who was a high U.S. governmental official, was accused by a defector from the communist party of having supplied the Russians with secret military information. The above evidence convincingly established that the documents in question (the so-called "Baltimore letters") had been typed on Hiss' well-worn Woodstock typewriter.

Observe, on the right, how various letters appeared on a new Woodstock typewriter. Then notice the evidence of the scarring and faulty alignment of the keys of the typewriter that produced the "Baltimore letters" and the similarity to Hiss' typewriter.

the kinds of presses, including offset lithography and letterpress systems, the quality of professional workmanship, and the typefaces available to the printing trade.

OTHER ASPECTS OF DOCUMENT EXAMINATIONS

Inks. A number of techniques exist to determine the kind of ink which was used to produce a writing. Among them are the use of reagents on the ink lines, the spectrographic method, various specialized photographic techniques, thin-layer chromatography and others.

Determinations of the precise age of ink are not easy to make, and they are seldom positive, although it is frequently possible to determine that the ink used to write some words or characters is of a different type and age from that of the remainder of the writing on a document. Extensive scientific literature exists on the sophisticated techniques which have been developed for the examination and identification of inks.

A fairly recent development in the study of inks in document examinations is the advent of the ball-point pen, introduced in this country in 1945. In a ball-point pen, a rotatable ball approximately one millimeter in diameter is held in place in a small socket that permits the ball to revolve freely at the base of a penlike instrument. Inside the pen is the "ink," consisting of coloring materials such as dyes or pigments dispersed in oil or another organic liquid. The ink flows down to the socket in which revolves the ball point. During writing, the rotating ball receives the writing fluid from the ink supply and deposits it on the paper.

Ball-point pen inks can also be analyzed by document examiners using a variety of techniques, among them thin-layer chromatography and infrared luminescence photography. Other writing traces, such as those produced by lead pencils, can also be examined by the experts. A new instrument has been introduced which utilizes a fiber-brush tip; it, too, produces a characteristic stroke.

Paper. The study of papers is a fundamental part of the document examiner's training, since the types and grades of paper are endless, going from ordinary writing paper, with its multitude of qualities, to wrapping paper, wax paper, cardboard and newsprint, to name but a few.

Investigations involving paper may answer the question of

whether the substance is in fact paper and of what quality or type. The identity of one piece of writing paper with that of a stack of pages may be determined by general composition, form dates, the thickness of the paper and sometimes even by a microscopic comparison of the cutting marks on the edge.

Some manufacturers change their watermarks yearly, and this practice affords a means by which the date of the paper's production may be ascertained. In many instances this fact alone can establish the invalidity of a document. For instance, if a will dated June 1, 1960, is written on paper that bears a watermark establishing that it was not produced until 1970, the will is obviously invalid, and for that reason alone.

While most of the techniques involved in the examination of paper require special knowledge, elaborate instrumentation and extensive experience, the observant policeman, though untrained in questioned document investigations, can often learn important facts from the study of a paper itself. In one case, a serious credibility question was raised when a witness told a police officer that she had written down certain facts on a piece of form paper in 1965, although the date code stamped at the bottom of the sheet indicated it had not been placed in circulation until 1969.

Examiner Qualifications

No firm guidelines can be given for achieving the qualifications required for proficiency in documentary examination. There are no academic programs or degrees to prepare one for a career in the field; there are even fewer training programs in questioned document examination than there are in other types of criminalistics specialties for which there is no formal course of study, such as fingerprint identification. Generally, one must be familiar with all of the rather extensive technical literature that exists in document examinations and have achieved practical experience under the guidance of an expert.

The required practical experience can therefore be acquired by working outside law enforcement, usually on the apprenticeship system. It is important to remember that the field of questioned document examination is one in which there are a great number of self-styled, inexperienced, so-called "handwriting experts" and "graphologists" who offer their services to attorneys and businesses.

Such individuals could not possibly be considered suitable teachers for the purpose of individualized training.

REFERENCES

Conway, *Evidential Documents*, Charles C Thomas, Publisher (Springfield), 1959.

Harrison, *Suspect Documents—Their Scientific Examination*, Praeger Publishers (New York), 1958.

Hilton, *Scientific Examination of Documents*, Callaghan & Company (Chicago), 1956.

Osborn, *Questioned Documents*, 2nd ed., Boyd Printing Company (Albany), 1929.

Osborn, *The Problem of Proof*, Boyd Printing Company (Albany), 1942.

Osborn, *Questioned Document Problems*, Boyd Printing Company (Albany), 1944.

Chapter 4

Firearms Evidence

Firearms evidence centers around fired bullets and shells, which are examined for the purpose of determining the type or make of guns from which they were fired, or for determining whether or not they were fired from a particular weapon. This activity is frequently called "ballistics," which is really a misnomer because the word "ballistics" is more properly applicable to the study of the trajectory of bullets or missiles rather than of the missiles and the missile launchers (bullets and guns) themselves. In the course of his activities, the firearms technician may find it necessary to study powder or shot patterns on clothing or on a body for the purpose of approximating from what distance a gun was fired. Occasionally, he is also called upon to restore the eradicated serial numbers on a gun and to perform other firearms-related tests.

Shotgun and Pistol or Rifle Differences

The extent and nature of the scientific aids available for a firearms case depend upon the kind of weapon involved. If it were a shotgun, the pellets in the body of a victim would not be useful (except in extremely rare cases) for purposes of identifying the gun from which they were fired. On the other hand, if the victim were shot with a pistol or a rifle, the bullet or bullets would probably enable the examiner to determine whether or not they were fired from the suspected weapon. The difference lies in the fact that the interior of a shotgun barrel is a smooth bore—without marks that can be impressed on the pellets—whereas the interior of a pistol or a
70

rifle has marks that are left on fired bullets. Shells discharged from automatic weapons may also provide an opportunity for weapon identification.

Understanding how bullets and shells can be identified as having come from a certain type and make of weapon, or from a specific weapon, depends upon some knowledge of how firearms are manufactured. We begin here with the manufacture of pistol and rifle barrels.

RIFLED BARREL MANUFACTURE

First, a hole is bored through a cylindrical bar of steel of the desired diameter for the particular weapon. That diameter determines the "caliber" of the weapon. It is expressed in hundredths (or thousandths) of an inch, or in millimeters. Therefore, a weapon with a bore diameter of forty-five hundredths of an inch would be a "forty-five" (.45) caliber gun. Likewise, a weapon of foreign manufacture possessing a bore diameter of nine millimeters is said to be a nine-millimeter (9 mm) caliber gun.

In earlier days, after the hole had been bored a "cutter" was used to scrape out twisting grooves, the "rifling" contour of the interior, which produced a high rotational velocity in a fired bullet, giving it gyroscopic stability and consequently greater accuracy, range and energy impact. But a bullet fired through a smooth-bore barrel travels in an end-over-end fashion. For an illustration of the twisting appearance of the interior of a rifled barrel, see Figure 28B.

"Cutters" have been replaced by what is known as a "broach," a long, hard, cylindrical, segmented tool that in one operation produces all of the twisting grooves desired by the manufacturer. As shown in Figure 28C, some manufacturers prefer four grooves, others five or six; and they may twist either to the right or to the left. The way in which the bullets themselves are affected is illustrated in Figure 28D and in Figure 29.

Regardless of the type of instrument used to produce the rifling within a barrel, each barrel inevitably acquires minute marks, primarily through minor accidental occurrences during the rifling process. They are not the same for any two barrels, even though manufactured one right after the other. The magnified photograph of a bullet in Figure 30 shows the kind of marks transmitted to the bullet by the structural characteristics of a barrel's interior.

CLASS CHARACTERISTICS

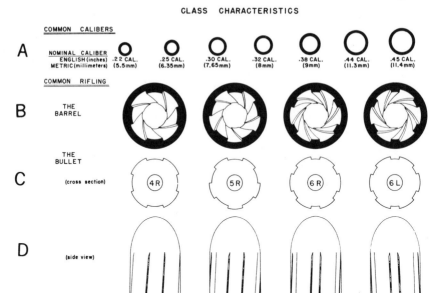

Figure 28. An illustration of how manufacturers' specifications for barrel making affect "class characteristics" which are the marks impressed on bullets fired through a barrel. Courtesy: Albert Biassoti, San Jose, Calif.

The individuality of each rifle barrel can best be appreciated by observing, in Figure 31, how great the differences are within the same barrel between its own grooves (and between the "lands"). A and B are two identical photographic prints, made from the same negative, of the entire circumference of a bullet fired from a barrel that was made by the original "cutter" process. The difference in appearance upon a first look at A and B is due to the fact that one

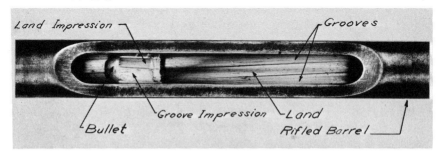

Figure 29. Barrel interior and bullet. Observe the twist in the grooves and in the projecting interspaces (the lands). Also note the groove and the land impressions on the bullet, which has been pushed through the unsectioned portion of the barrel to its present position. Courtesy: Charles M. Wilson, Madison, Wisconsin

Figure 30.

of the prints has been shifted over one postion, so that each land impression can be compared with the one adjacent to it. For instance, the photograph of groove 1 (G_1) in B is the same as groove 1 (G_1) in A, but it has been placed beneath groove 2 in order to more vividly demonstrate the difference between 1 and 2. The same is done for the other lands and grooves. Thus it may be observed how distinct the striations on each groove and on each land impression are from those on the adjoining grooves and lands. For example, observe the prominent striation on G_2 of A, which does not appear at all on G_1 of B, and also the one on L_2 of B, which is absent on L_3 of A. This comparison demonstrates that even within the same gun barrel there is no significant duplication of the characteristics on the various lands and grooves. Since that is true of every barrel, it may be appreciated how unlikely it would be to find two gun barrels (even though of successive manufacture in the same factory) that contain identical characteristics throughout their interiors.

In attaching significance to the similarity of individual character-

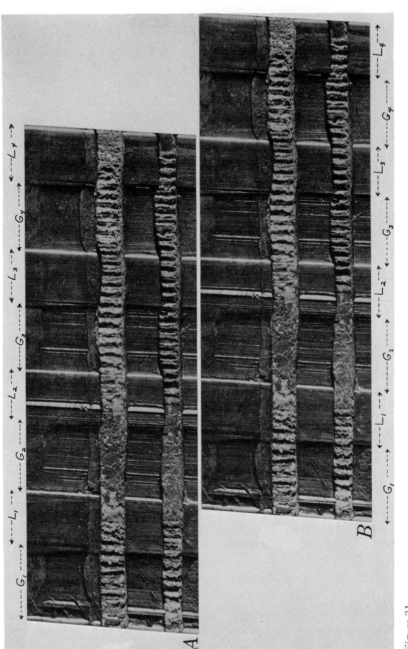

Figure 31.

istics on two bullets (for instance, one removed from the body of a murder victim and one fired from a suspected weapon) and in concluding that the same gun fired both bullets, a firearms examiner merely infers that in view of the coincidence of their many individual characteristics it is improbable that they could have been fired from different weapons. He can mathematically demonstrate the improbability of such a chance duplication and he can point out that no firearms technician has ever found two bullets fired from different guns which bore the same individual barrel marks.

IDENTIFYING FIRED BULLETS AND SHELLS

Because of manufacturers' different concepts concerning the preferred structure of the interior of a rifled barrel (for example, six grooves instead of four, or a twist to the left instead of to the right), a fired bullet may reveal to the expert the make of the gun from which it was fired. Sometimes precise measurements of the lands and grooves are needed to obtain such a clue, and there are of course instances when the expert can only exclude certain possibilities rather than point to a particular make. This is especially so with regard to some cheaper, foreign made products.

Since there is no practical way of making a comparison directly between the imperfections and irregularities within a barrel and the reverse impressions on a bullet, the technician fires a series of "test" bullets from the suspected weapon and then uses them instead of the gun barrel itself for comparison. In order to secure a comparison test bullet without damaging its individual characteristics or distorting its shape, the test bullet is fired into boxes filled with some soft material such as cotton waste. The test bullet might also be fired into a water container, called a bullet "recovery tank." After making a preliminary examination consisting of determining the test bullet's various class characteristics (lands, grooves, etc.), and if he finds them similar to those on the evidence bullet, the technician proceeds with a microscopic examination of the individual characteristics of both bullets.

He uses a binocular comparison microscope (see Figure 32), which is an instrument consisting essentially of two separate microscopes mounted side by side and fitted with a comparison bridge in which there is an arrangement of lenses and prisms that produces the effect of fusing the images of objects as they appear in the field

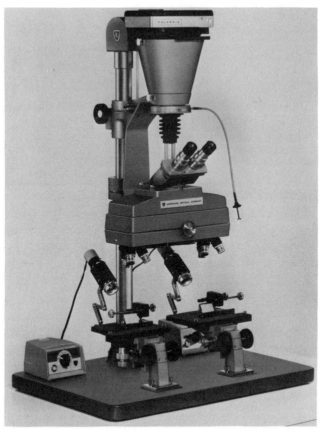

Figure 32. A modern binocular comparison microscope used by firearms examiners. Note the Polaroid camera mounted above the microscope for producing photomicrographs. Courtesy: American Optical Company

of each microscope. The evidence bullet is placed under one microscope and the test bullet under the other. The bullets are mounted horizontally by means of a plastic substance on cylindrical, adjustable holders.

After the two bullets are mounted, the usual practice is for the examiner to scrutinize the entire surface of the rotating bullets at relatively low magnifications for the purpose of locating on one of the bullets the most prominent group of striations. Once such marks are located, say on the evidence bullet, that bullet is permitted to remain stationary. Then the examiner rotates the other, or test, bullet in an attempt to find a corresponding area with individual characteristics that match those on the evidence bullet. If what appears to be a match is located, the examiner rotates both bullets simultaneously to determine whether or not similar coincidences exist on other portions of the bullets. Upon finding corresponding marks on other portions, while having the bullets in the same relative positions as when the first matches were observed, the examiner proceeds with further examinations of the same nature at higher magnifications. A careful study of all the detail on both bullets ultimately permits him to conclude that both bullets were or were not fired through the same barrel. Figure 33 illustrates how two bullets fired through the same barrel appear when viewed through the comparison microscope. The photographs show portions of the evidence and test bullets side by side (separated by a fine hairline in each illustration) with characteristics on both bullets in match position.

Even if bullets were fired in succession from the same weapon, not all individual characteristics would be identical. There would be some striations caused by powder residues, rust, corrosion and pitting, sand or dirt, and other surface factors or "fugitive" materials which of course are not likely to be duplicated on all bullets

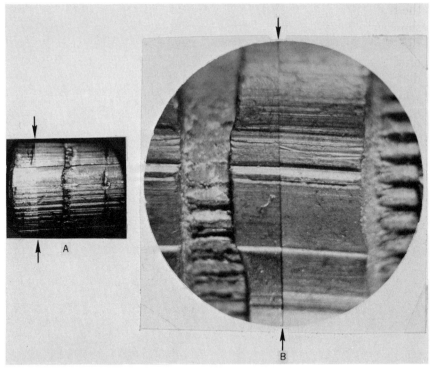

Figure 33. A is a photomicrograph, taken through a binocular comparison microscope, showing two bullets in match position at relatively low magnification. B illustrates the match position of only a small portion of the same bullets at high magnification.

fired through that particular barrel. Moreover, there might be other striations on the bullets which would have no relationship to the interior of the barrel through which they were fired. For instance, there might be marks on metal-cased bullets due to imperfections on the interior of the sizing die used in the fabrication of the bullet. Likewise, fired bullets might contain crimp or burr impressions left there by the mouth of the cartridge case or shell. Obviously, the presence or absence of such marks, whether duplicated or not, must be discounted by the firearms identification technician.

While distorted evidence bullets often make identification difficult, they do not invariably preclude an identification of the weapon through which they were fired. Figure 34 illustrates such a case. On the left is a bullet fragment removed from a victim's body. The bullet had previously penetrated the sheet metal hood of an automobile, the metal partition between the driver's compartment and the motor, and the dashboard. The bullet in the center is a test bullet fired from the suspected weapon. The bullet fragment and the test bullet were photographed at the same scale. To the right is shown a photomicrograph showing a matching of the striations on the evidence bullet (left portion of the photomicrograph) with those on the test bullet. Due to the bent and twisted condition of the evidence bullet fragment, not all of the land impressions were in focus when the photomicrograph was taken, which accounts for the blurred area on the lower left portion of the picture.

Since bullets are cylindrical and since a bullet that has entered or

Figure 34. Identification of a bullet fragment.

gone through a body has fewer, defined barrel impressions than the one previously shown in Figure 30, many firearms experts are unwilling to use comparison microscope photographs when testifying in court. The out-of-focus areas are hard to explain to jurors, and defense attorneys harp on this deficiency in an effort to discredit the witness; hence the usual reliance upon opinion testimony by the expert, unaided by photographs.

Although constituting valuable evidence in some cases, shell identification is not nearly so useful as bullet identification, for two reasons. First, unless the shell was ejected or discarded at or near the scene of the crime, its identification as coming from a particular gun is of little or no probative value. Second, even if a shell found at or near the scene is identified as having been fired from a suspect's weapon, that fact does not establish, as does a bullet, that it was the gun used in the offense. But the characteristic marks made on shells by the parts of a gun are individualistic.

The "breech block," which supports the head of a cartridge as it is fired, is a tooled piece of steel on which individual, accidental marks are left during manufacture. Also during the manufacturing process, individual marks are acquired by a gun's firing pin and, in the case of an automatic weapon, by its "ejector" and "extractor." (See Figure 35 for an illustration of the location of these parts and for an indication of the mechanics involved in the firing of a cartridge in an automatic weapon.) All of these parts are capable of leaving telltale impressions on fired shells, most frequently the face of the breech block. Sometimes the magazine clips of an automatic weapon, or the chambers of a revolver, may also leave marks on shells. Shell identifications are of course made by using the same scientific procedures previously described for bullet identification: the marks made by gun parts on a crime scene shell are compared under a binocular microscope with the part marks on a shell that has been test-fired from a suspected weapon. (For an illustration of gun identification by means of firing pin marks, see Figure 36.)

DETERMINING DISTANCE OF SHOT

Differentiating among accident, self-defense, suicide and criminal homicide in a shooting case may hinge on an expert determination of the distance between the gun muzzle and the first surface of the victim, clothing or skin. Besides the shot or bullet, other important

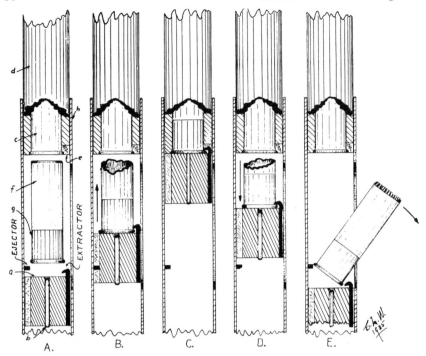

Figure 35. An illustration of the action involved in the firing of a cartridge in an automatic weapon.

In A, the small *a* identifies the face of the breech block; *b*, the firing pin. The vertical labels identify the ejector and extractor. In B, the breech mechanism carrying the hook (extractor) pushes the shell forward into the chamber. In C, the breech is closed and locked in firing position. D shows the extractor engaged with the shell head and the breech traveling to the rear after firing. E illustrates how the left side of the shell strikes the ejector, casting the shell to the right and out of the chamber. Courtesy: Charles M. Wilson, Madison, Wisconsin

elements are projected from the muzzle of the gun at the time of firing. Flame, finely divided metal, carbon, partially burned and un-burned powder and grease are thrown out for distances varying with each component's physical properties. The pattern observed may represent a composite of some or all of these fractions.

At close range, say from zero to two inches, gases hot enough to scorch and sear belch from the muzzle. A microscopic examination of the region around the wound will disclose the effects of this phe-nomenon. Fibers of cloth will show thermal changes; hair may be blistered and the skin itself burned.

At distances farther away, scorching ceases and a black smudge composed of carbon, powder particles and fine metal particles can be seen. The velocity of the fine material rapidly diminishes at greater distances, approximately six to ten inches, and this material does not contact the skin or clothing with sufficient force to stick; it simply disperses into the air. At this range, only the larger, heavier powder grains, fair-sized particles of metal and grease continue on to end up on the surface surrounding the bullet hole. Of course, in each preceding stage, the pattern possesses all of the elements not eliminated by distance; in fact, the particles capable of distant projection possess the ability to penetrate at closer distances and can be found embedded in clothing or skin.

Finally, a point is reached at which the velocity of all except the projectile has diminished so much that they will not adhere to or reach the surface surrounding the bullet hole. It is this limiting distance that is most crucial. If it can be established that the maximum distance for powder deposit exceeds the reach of the arms of the victim, then the absence of a powder pattern clearly indicates that the shooter and victim were outside the range of physical contact when the shot was fired. Although other mitigating circumstances

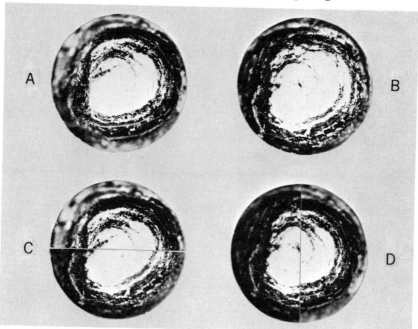

Figure 36. A shows the firing pin impressions on an evidence shell; B shows the impressions on a test shell. C and D show the coincidence of the impressions as half of A and half of B are placed alongside of each other.

might indicate otherwise, such an established fact usually eliminates self-destruction or an accidental discharge during a struggle.

The determination of the distance from muzzle to surface cannot be reduced to a formula or table; in fact, what actually occurs is only an approximation. Although the cloud of gaseous discharge forms a roughly cone-shaped figure, the spread, shape and density of the pattern depend on many factors. Different combinations of gun and ammunition influence the pattern at any given distance. Any factor or variable which affects the burning rate and pressure characteristics of gun powders may result in a powder pattern variance. Thus variations in the length of the barrel, the gap between cylinder and barrel, and the fit of the bullet in the barrel may change the pattern even though the weapon tested is of the same make and model as that which produced the "crime" pattern. In fact, even ammunition of the same make but of different manufactured lots can produce variations in spread and density of pattern, even when fired from the same gun. Consequently, evidence of this nature must be accepted with reservation.

When a victim displays a powder pattern on the skin, the pattern should be photographed with a scale or ruler placed in the plane of the powder pattern at the edge of the field of view. This will permit later reproduction of the pattern full size for comparison with test patterns. Failure to detect a substantial visible pattern should lead to the use of infrared photography and chemical detectors; in extreme cases, skin surrounding the wound can be removed during the autopsy and examined by soft X rays.

When a suspected gun is obtained, as well as ammunition of the same type and brand as was used to produce the shot pattern on the victim, a series of firings can produce test patterns for comparison purposes, as shown in Figure 37. By comparing the test patterns with the pattern found on the victim or on some other object, an examiner may find a similarity in pattern formation that may enable him to approximate the distance at which the shot was fired.

GUNSHOT RESIDUE TESTS

Many times it would be extremely helpful if a determination could be made, by means of a scientific examination of a suspect's body, and particularly of his hands, of whether or not he had re-

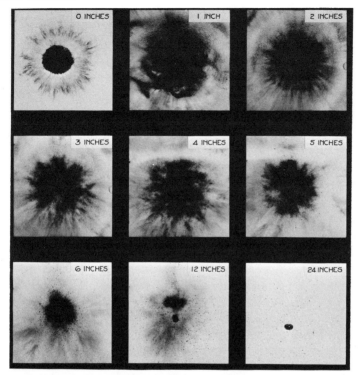

Figure 37. Shot patterns on white blotting paper.

cently fired a gun. In 1933 Theodoro Gonzales of Mexico announced that he had developed a test that could provide such evidence. It was known as the "diphenylamine paraffin test" and consisted of making a paraffin cast of one or both of a suspect's hands and then treating the inside area of the cast with drops of a chemical (diphenylamine in a concentrated solution of sulphuric acid); if a reaction occurred in the form of dark blue pinpoint specks, it was considered evidence of recent gun firing. The theory behind the test was that the results established the presence of particles of nitrates or nitrites, deposited on the hand by the gases of a discharged cartridge. The flaw in this theory, however, was that similar reactions could result from the presence of other, innocently acquired substances containing nitrates or nitrites, as was disclosed by controls conducted in various criminalistics laboratories. But the search has continued for a reliable, specific test for gunpowder ingredients that are not likely to be found on a person's hands from any other source. Recently developed tests of this nature offer considerable promise. Though not yet perfected, they may still serve as an investigative aid, if not as legal proof of recent gun firing.

Restoring Obliterated Serial Numbers

Investigators sometimes encounter firearms from which the serial numbers have been filed off to make tracing the guns more difficult. Sometimes even a false number may have been stamped in as a replacement. It is occasionally possible, through various chemical techniques, to reveal the number that has been eradicated. In Figure 38, for example, the left portion of the illustration shows how a gun appeared to the naked eye after the serial number had been removed. The right portion of the photograph shows how the number was revealed after an etching process.

One process for restoring obliterated serial numbers requires cleaning the area with fine emery paper and then swabbing it with a strong acid solution composed of 40 cc of concentrated hydrochloric acid, 30 cc of distilled water, 25 cc of ethyl alcohol and 5

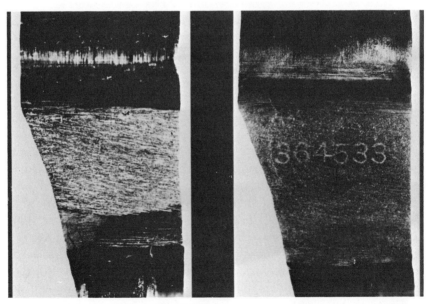

Figure 38. Before and after views of the restoration of obliterated serial numbers on a gun by the chemical etching process.

grams of cupric chloride, which is rubbed onto the surface already wet with the solution.

Similar techniques exist for the restoration of serial numbers on aluminum, a material increasingly used in the manufacture of engines, power tools and even firearms. The standard reagents used in etching on iron and other metals provide too vigorous a reaction with aluminum, resulting in pitted metal and blurred results. For that reason, special dilute solutions are applied to aluminum surfaces, using metallic mercury as a catalyst.

FIREARMS IDENTIFICATION EXPERTISE

Firearms investigation and examination is another field of specialty for which, as for fingerprinting and the examination of questioned documents, there are no degree programs in colleges or universities. So most of the training of firearms examiners must come once again from "within the ranks" through the apprenticeship system and through a study of the voluminous technical literature. However, because of the large technical and advisory staffs of the many firearms and ammunition manufacturers, and because of the frequency with which firearms feature in civil litigation which involves accidental deaths and firearms malfunctions that cause injury, there are a number of highly qualified firearms experts in this country who are not associated with law enforcement agencies. They make their services available to plaintiffs and defendants in civil cases and, occasionally, in criminal cases.

When a law enforcement agency is not equipped to handle firearms cases, it can, as with fingerprints and questioned documents, appeal for assistance to the FBI crime laboratory. Suggestions for the handling, collecting and transporting of firearms evidence are given in the FBI guidelines printed in the appendix.

PRESENTING EVIDENCE IN COURT

American courts now freely admit testimony on all of the generally accepted aspects of firearms identification, provided that the witness has been properly qualified and that a proper foundation has been laid for the admissibility of the evidence. In presenting testimony in court, firearms experts occasionally use enlarged photographs and photomicrographs of the type used to illustrate this chapter. But it should be remembered that the complexities involved in understanding and properly interpreting photomicrographs have led some experts to believe that such exhibits tend to confuse, rather than explain, a witness's conclusions. Therefore, it is not unusual for the firearms examiner who qualifies as an expert to give his conclusions without illustrative exhibits.

REFERENCES

Burrard, *The Identification of Firearms and Forensic Ballistics*, Herbert Jenkins, Ltd. (London), 1951.

Davis, *An Introduction to Tool Marks, Firearms and the Striagraph*, Charles C Thomas, Publisher (Springfield), 1958.

Gunther, *The Identification of Firearms*, John Wiley & Sons (New York), 1935.

Hatcher, Jury and Weller, *Firearms Investigation, Identification and Evidence*, The Stackpole Company (Harrisburg), 1957.

Matthews, *Firearms Identification*, The University of Wisconsin Press (Madison), 1962.

Smith, *Small Arms of the World*, The Stackpole Company (Harrisburg), 1962.

Stebbins, *Pistols—A Modern Encyclopedia*, The Stackpole Company (Harrisburg), 1962.

Chapter 5

Tool Mark Comparisons

Tools or other implements used for cutting metal or for turning or prying objects apart usually have serrated edges or nicks on those edges. Those in turn often leave impressions of one sort or another on the material to which they are applied. The obvious gross impressions may only indicate the nature of the tool or implement used, but minute impressions may also be left which can be of great value in determining whether or not they were or were not made by a particular tool. The science by which such determinations can be made is called "comparative micrography."

The term may be applied to almost any type of case in which a hard object is applied to a softer object that is capable of absorbing marks present on the harder one. For instance, if a metal implement is used on wood with a protective coating, or perhaps even in the grain line area of raw wood, it may be possible to identify the implement that was used. But the greatest potential for comparative micrography is where hard implements such as tools are applied to other metals, as so frequently happens in burglary cases.

An excellent illustration of the type of case in which the expert in comparative micrography can be of great assistance to the police investigator is a case in which bolt cutters have been used in the course of a burglary to remove a window bar or to cut a chain or other such object. For the purpose of determining whether or not a bolt cutter found in the suspect's possession was the tool used, a piece of lead is cut by the suspected cutter in order to obtain a specimen of the characteristics of its cutting edge. The severed end of the bolt or the cut link of a chain, or whatever else may have been cut, is then placed under one barrel of a binocular comparison microscope and the cut area of the lead plate is placed under the other barrel, as is shown in Figure 39A. If a number of the impressions converge, as in the photograph taken through the comparison microscope illustrated in Figure 39B, the conclusion can be drawn that the suspected instrument was the one used in the burglary.

The proper interpretation of what is shown in a photomicrograph must be left up to the expert, for laymen looking at the photograph are often confounded by what appear to be dissimilarities. In Figure 39B, for instance, the seeming dissimilarity in the lower part of the picture is due to the curved surface of the cut end of the bolt and the consequent lack of identical lens focus upon it and the lead plate.

Crowbars frequently leave impressions on metal objects that permit a determination to be made as to whether or not a suspected crowbar was responsible for those impressions. Such a case is

Figure 39A.

Figure 39B. Left portion: bolt; right portion: test lead plate.

graphically illustrated in Figure 40. A is a photograph of a jimmied door; B is a suspected crowbar. The marks on the strike plate that is attached to the whitened area of the wall are clearly observable in A. Figure 40C is a photomicrograph of the results of a comparison between the impressions on the strike plate and those made by the suspected crowbar on the test lead plate.

Although certain match areas in C do not appear to be clear to the novice, the skilled technician has no doubt that the same crowbar was used in both instances. The areas in the picture which seem to reveal a nonmatch of the impressions are due to the fact that the laboratory lead specimen was obtained as a result of a continuous stroking of the edge of the crowbar on the lead plate, whereas the marks left on the strike plate were caused by uneven pressure and by a bending of the metal, hence showing some void areas in the left center portion of the photograph. This again illustrates why

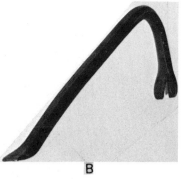

Figure 40A and B.

Figure 40C. The left portion is the strike plate; the right portion is the test lead plate.

many comparative micrography experts, like many firearms identification experts, do not always use photomicrographs as demonstrative evidence when they are called upon to testify in court. Instead,
they explain the test procedures they have followed and the conclusions they have reached, without using illustrative exhibits.

A simple tool such as a screwdriver may leave telltale impressions
on metal objects with which it comes in contact. In Figure 41, for
example, a case is illustrated in which a screwdriver was used to
pry loose a lock by wedging the end of the tool against the strike
plate and applying the pressure needed to open the door. A shows a
photograph of the door pried ajar with the screwdriver. B shows
part of the lock bearing impressions left by the screwdriver. C is the
suspected tool. Photomicrograph D discloses a great similarity between the impressions on the lock and those left on the test lead
plate by the suspected screwdriver.

The full potential of comparative micrography is such that it may
be possible in some instances even to identify a drill as being the
one used to open a lock on burglarized premises. Figure 42A shows
a comparison microscope with tumbler lock, thought to have been
opened by the suspected drill, placed under one of its barrels. A
test plate in which holes were made by the same drill is under
the other barrel. Figure 42B is the resulting photomicrograph,

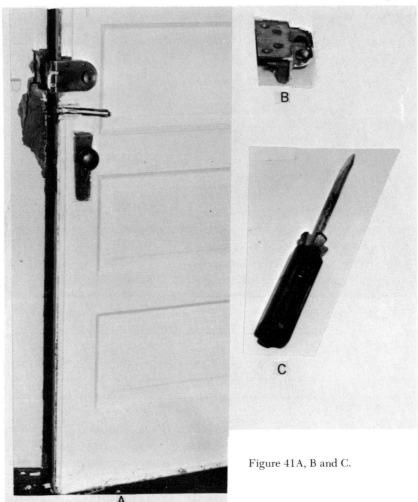

Figure 41A, B and C.

showing the matching of the drill impressions on the lock with those on the test lead plate.

As is evident from the foregoing illustrations, the opinion of a comparative micrography expert can be supported by presenting demonstrative evidence to a judge or jury in the nature of photomicrographs when photographs will indeed assist the fact finders at the trial in understanding the nature and importance of the expert's conclusions.

Resort to comparative micrography techniques may also be made in less complicated examinations, as when a comparison is made be-

Figure 41D. Left portion: Strike plate; right portion: test lead plate.

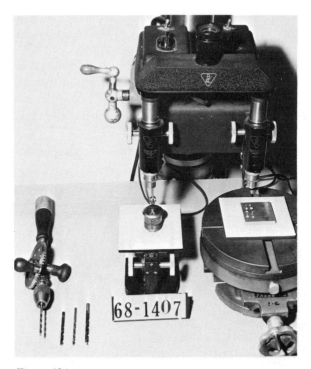

Figure 42A.

Figure 42B. Left portion: the lock; right portion: the test lead plate.

tween a piece of broken metal found at the scene of an automobile accident and the remnant of it on a suspected vehicle. It may also be used as regards cut or torn objects, as illustrated in Figure 43. On top is shown a piece of the cut hose from an automobile engine alongside one from an engine suspected of being the stolen one. On the bottom is the photomicrograph illustrating the similarity of detail between the cut ends.

Although not strictly within the area of comparative microgra-

Figure 43.

PIN TUMBLER LOCK

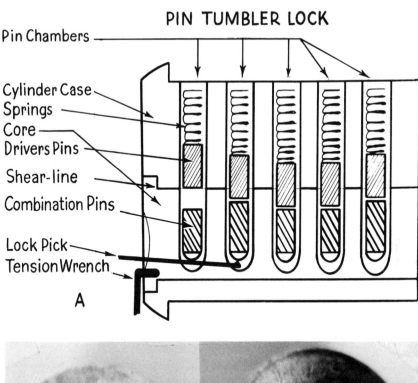

Pin Chambers

Cylinder Case
Springs
Core
Drivers Pins

Shear-line

Combination Pins

Lock Pick
Tension Wrench

A

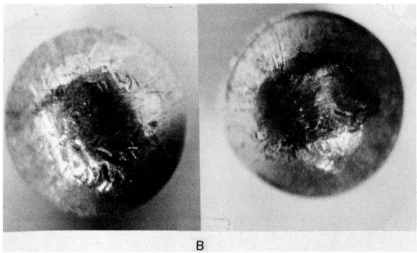

B

Figure 44.

phy, some reference must be made to the matter of ascertaining whether or not entrance to a building was in fact effected by force or as a result of occupant neglect. A resolution of this issue is of two-fold importance in instances where there is no obvious evidence of forcible entry: for police purposes and for insurance determination purposes.

A skillfully "picked" lock may not have any obvious outward marks, but a microscopic examination can be very revealing. Picking a pin tumbler lock is not a difficult task, as Figure 44A illustrates. First of all, a tension wrench is used to turn the core off the center. Then a lock pick is inserted to raise the pins out of the core and onto its shoulder, thereby permitting the door to be opened. Although there is usually no outward indication of such an operation, the lock itself can be disassembled and the combination pins examined for pick marks. Figure 44B shows how such pick marks appear when examined under magnification.

Comparative micrography is fully accepted in the field of science and the courts readily admit the testimony of a qualified expert after proper authentication of the exhibits upon which he bases his testimony.

Chapter 6

Small Objects and Particles Comparison

The expert microscopic analysis of small objects and particles—the science of microanalysis—can serve three primary functions: (1) an investigative aid in the apprehension of a criminal offender; (2) the elimination of innocent suspects; and (3) the establishment of guilt or innocence in the courtroom. In the gathering of such physical evidence, four considerations are of the utmost importance: (1) the evidence must not be contaminated or altered; (2) it must be properly marked and identified; (3) the chain of possession must be minimized and recorded; and (4) it should be submitted to the expert—the microanalyst—as soon as possible.

HAIR

Hair found at the scene of a crime, or on the body of the victim of a crime of violence, can be of considerable value when properly collected, preserved and delivered to a police laboratory microanalyst. A simple illustration is the case in which a struggle occurred between a victim and the offender, such as a rape-murder. Hair may have been pulled from the offender's head. Its color alone may furnish a valuable investigative lead. Then, after the apprehension of a suspect, a microscopic comparison can be made to determine similarity or dissimilarity to the suspect's hair. Likewise, hair may be found on an object possessed by a criminal suspect or upon his own body which is different from his own and which may be compared with the victim's hair specimens.

Although there is no known way of positively identifying hair as

97

having come from a particular person, demonstrating the similarity of color, structure, pigmentation and other characteristics can help to prove guilt when considered along with other evidence against the suspect or accused person (see Figure 45).

Bearing in mind the potential of hair analysis and comparison, the investigator should attempt to locate and preserve whatever hair may have been left at the scene or on the victim, and he should also obtain specimens from the victim.

When hair is found on an article of clothing or on some other object it is a good idea to preserve the clothing or object itself along with the hair, which should be permitted to remain in as undis-

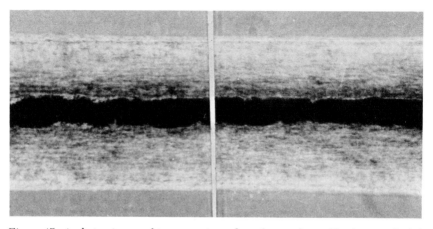

Figure 45. A photomicrographic comparison of two human hairs. The hair on the left was recovered from the clothing of a hit-and-run victim; the hair on the right was embedded in the auto used in the suspected hit-and-run.

turbed a position as circumstances permit. Hair specimens, whether removed from the clutched hands of a murder victim or obtained from the body of a suspect, should be placed in a *clean* pillbox, vial or envelope. (If an envelope is used the hair should first be placed in clean paper.)

Hair recovered from different locations or sources should be placed in separate containers rather than lumped together in a single container. The specimens should be handled as little as possible because there may be trace materials (blood or dust, for instance) on the hair that could be of value to the microanalyst. Each container should be sealed to prevent loss, alteration or contamination, and each should be suitably marked for future identification purposes. The more detailed the information is, the easier the task of tracing an exhibit in order to have it admitted in evidence at a trial becomes.

Hair specimens obtained for comparison purposes should be representative samples. For instance if head hairs appear to be involved, specimens should be taken from the top, rear and front of the head, as well as from the sides and neck, because there may be no way for the investigator to know at the time which particular area was the source of the hair with which comparisons are to be ultimately made. Hair specimens obtained for comparison purposes should be *pulled out* so as to recover the entire hair shaft. If they cannot be pulled out they should be cut as close to the root as possible.

In sex offense cases, hair found on the body of the victim may be either head hairs or pubic hairs; consequently, when specimens are obtained from a suspect they should consist of hair from both regions of the body (see Figure 46).

Where hair from an animal is needed for comparison with other animal hairs (as when a dog has attacked a burglar and dog hairs are found on a suspect's clothing), samples should be taken from all of the major parts of the animal's body. Incidentally, the structure,

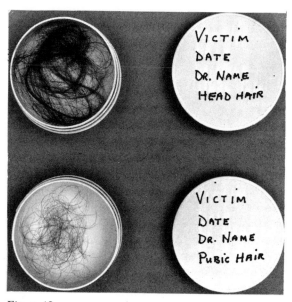

Figure 46.

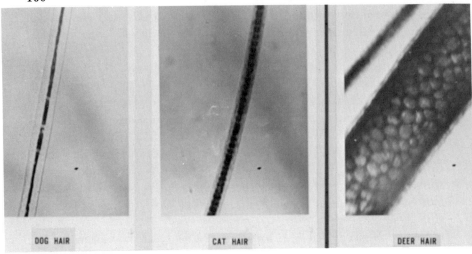

DOG HAIR   CAT HAIR   DEER HAIR

Figure 47.

pigmentation distribution and other characteristics of animal hairs differ from those of other animals, and from man, and a microanalyst's examination of a hair can identify the kind of animal from which it came. Figure 47 shows hair differences among several animals.

FIBERS

Fibers from clothing and other articles may play as important a role as hair in a case investigation. They, too, may have been left on the body or clothing of a victim or elsewhere at the scene of a crime.

Fibers may be of various origins: cotton, hemp, asbestos, fiber glass, nylon, orlon, and so on. They are all of a different consistency and therefore identifiable as to the kind of material.

Fibers of value to the microanalyst may be found in a victim's hands, under his fingernails and in or on other parts of the body or clothing. They may also be found in or on motor vehicles (for example, in the trunk of a car in a kidnapping or murder case, or underneath a hit-and-run vehicle); on weapons such as knives, clubs and firearms; on fired bullets that have penetrated clothing; or embedded in blood, tissue, semen or other bodily substances.

The potential of fiber examination is illustrated in Figure 48, where cloth fibers on a murder weapon (a pair of scissors) possessed by a suspect, or discarded by him, were determined to be morphologically similar to those fibers associated with the victim. Such evidence, standing alone, may seem inconsequential, but when considered along with related evidence it may be of considerable value.

One cardinal rule for investigators to follow is to submit to the microanalyst, whenever possible, the *entire* article (for example, the dress of a victim) on which fibers have been observed. Any such article should be placed in a plastic bag or other container *all by itself*. An intermingling of various articles may destroy whatever value each one may have had, particularly when the clothing of a victim is placed in the same receptacle as the clothing of a suspect.

When the fibers themselves are recovered by the investigator, as when taken from an automobile in a hit-and-run case, they should be placed in a *clean* pill box, vial or envelope (after being wrapped in paper) and the container should then be properly labeled. Here again, it is of great importance that there be no lumping together of fibers recovered from different sources.

Recovered fibers should not be handled any more than is absolutely necessary; otherwise, trace materials such as soil and paint flakes might be lost or contaminated.

Following is a listing of the reasons why investigators should look for and carefully preserve fiber materials:

A. Fibers present on a weapon may help to establish that the weapon was the one used in the particular crime

Figure 48. Fibers embedded in blood on scissors used in a homicide. The scissors were recovered from the auto of the suspect. Blood on the scissors was of the same blood group as the victim's, and fibers were of the same color and type as the fibers of the victim's sweater.

B. Fibers present on a fired bullet may establish that the bullet penetrated a certain garment or garments

C. Fibers present on a vehicle may establish that a particular vehicle was involved in a hit-and-run case

D. The presence of trace materials on fibers may tend to indicate the offender's environment or occupation and lead to his apprehension

E. Fibers present on the body or clothing of the victim of an assault, rape or homicide may help to identify the assailant

F. The interchange of fibers between two individuals may tend to establish physical contact between the two

G. The presence of fibers at a crime scene may tend to indicate the color of the clothing of the perpetrator, which may be an important investigative aid

H. Deposits of blood or semen may be present on fibers and may result in determining the blood group or the isolation of spermatozoa, which may prove to be important in the investigation of a crime

I. The condition of damaged fibers may reveal information about the type of instrument that caused the damage to the fiber as a wound was inflicted

J. Fibers from stolen furs may be present in or on the clothing of a suspect and may thereby tend to establish his connection with the incident.

GLASS

Glass fragments may be of great value in the investigation of many criminal offenses. In some instances the breaking of glass during the commission of a crime may be the result of an intentional act; in others, the result of an accidental occurrence. An illustration of the former is the breaking of the window of an automobile or a building to steal something within it. An illustration of an accidental occurrence is the breaking of a glass object such as a lamp during the course of a struggle between a criminal and his victim. In either type of situation, glass fragments may become embedded in the offender's clothing or deposited in his pocket or pant cuff; or fragments may become lodged in the implement used in an intentional breaking, as illustrated in Figure 49. Broken headlight glass at the scene of a hit-and-run accident frequently affords an opportunity to identify the involved vehicle.

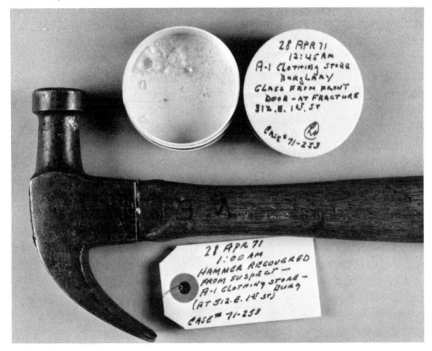

Figure 49. Glass recovered from the scene of a burglary (in pillbox) and glass fragments embedded in a hammer recovered from the tools of a suspect can be compared for physical and chemical properties to show that the glass embedded in the hammer came from the broken window at the crime scene.

The physical and chemical properties of glass fragments may be compared with those of the broken glass at the scene of the crime and a determination thereby made as to whether or not the fragments came from that source.

The comparison of glass fragments for a common source of origin is based on a series of tests utilizing microscopy and other instrumentation to determine the physical and chemical properties of the glass. The refractive index of the glass fragments is first determined microscopically. The refractive index is based on the fact that light travels through air at a greater velocity than through glass. When light enters the glass at an angle, some of the light waves enter the glass ahead of others, causing a bending of the beam. The amount of bending of the light wave in entering the glass is dependent upon the ratio between the speed of light in air and its speed in the glass. If both glass fragments bend the light entering them to the same degree, they are considered to have the same refractive index.

Another physical property of glass is measured microscopically through the use of a technique known as dispersion staining. By placing the glass in an oil of known refractive index and a refractive index near to that of the glass, introducing white light and observing it through a special microscope objective, the interface at the edges between the glass and liquid will appear colored. The color will be that for which the refractive indices of the glass and liquid are the same. If further modifications are made in the microscope objective, the complementary colors may also be studied. This method determines whether two glass fragments disperse white light similarly.

A third method used in comparing glass fragments is to determine their densities. Liquids of different densities are placed in a glass tube that is closed at one end. The heavier liquids are at the bottom of the tube and the lighter liquids toward the top. The two glass particles are introduced into the tube and if both come to rest (float) at the same point in the tube they are said to have equal densities.

A fourth method of testing the glass is to determine the chemical components of the glass through spectrographic analysis. The glass is burned at a very high temperature and each chemical element produces characteristic wavelengths of light when burned. These wavelengths are recorded on film from which the chemical composition of the glass can be determined.

As with hair and fibers, the potential of glass comparisons will be lost unless, first, the investigator makes a proper effort to locate the evidence and, second, employs the proper methods to preserve what he finds. An example of what should be looked for and how it should be preserved was shown earlier in Figure 49.

When fairly large pieces of glass are recovered, as at a hit-and-run accident scene, if the investigator readily observes how they fit together he may tape them into position and attach them to cardboard or other such material and then place everything in a suitable container to prevent further breakage in the process of delivering them to the laboratory technician. Where the fitting together of the pieces is not readily apparent, they should be carefully placed in a box, or double strength plastic bag, or other appropriate container.

A suspect's clothing which appears to contain glass fragments should, if possible, be delivered to the laboratory technician intact so that he himself may recover the fragments and at the same time search for other traces of evidence. When that cannot be done the fragments should be removed by the use of forceps, if any are available. Transparent tape can also be used in many instances. Lacking such facilities, the investigator can of course use his fingers. In all instances, the recovered fragments should be placed in a clean pillbox, vial or envelope, sealed and labeled for safe preservation and subsequent indentification purposes. When more than one glass object has been broken at the scene of the crime, glass from each object should be placed in a separate container.

PAINT

Paint as evidence is usually associated with burglaries, hit-and-run cases and other crimes involving the use of vehicles. However, the importance of paint as physical evidence should not be overlooked in other cases.

Paint is either removed from or transferred to an object, or both removed from and transferred to an object. Generally speaking, paint is recovered in the form of chips or smears. Oil-base paint is usually recovered in the form of smears, and automobile paint in the form of chips. The criminal may have paint on his clothing from the scene, as when paint is deposited on his clothing as a result of using force or a tool or other implement to enter an automobile or a home or to open a safe or cabinet. If the tool or implement has a painted surface, paint from it may be found superimposed on a painted object at the scene or embedded in the wood or metal of the object with which the tool came in contact. When an assault occurs and a painted object is used as the weapon, paint particles may be present on the clothing of the victim or embedded in his wounds.

In the investigation of hit-and-run accidents, the scene should be thoroughly searched for paint particles that may have been left there as a result of the impact between the pedestrian and auto or between two or more cars. In addition, the clothing of the victim should be submitted to the microanalyst as soon as possible so that the garments can be examined for the presence of paint particles which could be compared with paint samples from the suspect vehicle (see Figure 50).

In cases in which there is no suspect vehicle, an examination and analysis of the paint particles left at the scene can sometimes lead

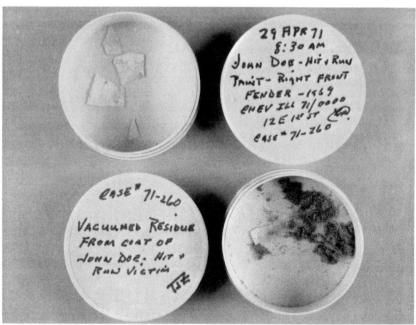

Figure 50. Paint recovered at a hit-and-run scene, compared with paint found in vacuumed residue from the clothing of a victim and discovered to be similar in physical and chemical properties, can help to establish that the vehicle was involved in the accident.

to the manufacturer, who might be able to tell what type of autos were coated in a particular year with that type of paint. In automobile accidents involving two cars there is usually a transfer of paint between them which may definitely establish that the two vehicles had come in contact. In cases in which a truck was used to remove merchandise from a warehouse, paint from the truck may have been deposited on the loading dock. In cases involving forcible entry, all tools in the possession of the suspect should be submitted to the microanalyst to be examined for paint that may be similar to the paint present on objects at the scene of the incident.

In the recovery of paint particles or stains, care must be exercized so as not to lose or destroy evidence such as hairs, fibers, soil or other trace materials. The paint should be chipped loose with a toothpick and placed in a clean pillbox, envelope or vial and suitably marked. Preferably, a wooden applicator such as a toothpick should be used to chip loose the paint rather than a metal object such as a knife or razor blade. Minute fragments of the metal from the knife or razor blade may become embedded in the paint and affect analysis. Paint chips may also be removed through the use of transparent pressure-sensitive tape. Whenever possible, all weapons with painted surfaces should be submitted to the microanalyst and no effort should be made by the field investigator to remove any paint present on such objects. The weapon should be placed in a plastic bag or other suitable container and sealed so that any paint that may fall off it will remain in the container and can be recovered.

No effort should be made to remove paint embedded in or superimposed on garments. Each garment to be examined should be placed in a clean plastic bag or other suitable container, sealed, properly marked and submitted to the microanalyst.

In recovering paint from an automobile, the inside of the fender or door may be tapped lightly and the paint chips from the outer surface may, if they are loose, fall, be collected on a clean piece of paper, and then placed in a suitable container. Or they may be removed through the use of transparent pressure-sensitive tape.

In assault and homicide cases, the body of the victim and his wounds should be thoroughly searched for the presence of paint particles that may have come from the weapon used to inflict the wounds. A good way to remove these particles is by transparent pressure-sensitive tape (as shown in Figure 51), or, if the particles are large, fingers may be used to recover the paint.

Paint embedded in fired bullets may establish that the victim was struck by a bullet that ricocheted off a wall or other painted surface before striking the victim, as for example when a warning shot was fired.

The importance of paint analysis is such that it may establish that a particular person was at a particular scene, that a certain automobile struck a certain individual or another automobile or stationary object, that a weapon was responsible for inflicting an injury, or that a specific tool or instrument was used to effect a forcible entry.

The identification and comparison of paint is usually accomplished through microscopic examinations, chemical solubility tests and instrumentation. In many cases where the paint particles to be compared contain a number of layers of paint, the microscopic determination that the pigment, pigment distribution, number of layers and sequence of layers are the same in both samples may be suf-

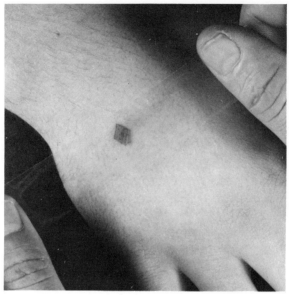

Figure 51.

ficient to identify their source. In situations where there is only one
layer of paint, chemical solubility tests may determine the type of
paint, and spectrographic analysis can disclose the chemical elements present. In addition, infrared-spectrophotometric examinations of the paint can reveal its components. Paint may also be de-
composed by heat (pyrolysis) and its gaseous products analyzed by
a gas chromatograph.

Soil

Soil is present at every crime scene in one form or another and is
usually recovered as a heterogeneous mixture which may include
clay, sand, rocks, black dirt, coal, plant material and other debris.
Soil is usually associated with cases involving outdoor crime scenes
but it may also feature in indoor scenes.

In many instances soil is either deposited at or carried away from
a crime scene. It may be transported on the shoes, clothing or body
of an individual from a specific location. It may be recovered at the
scene of an auto accident or hit-and-run incident where, due to the
impact of the auto with a pedestrian, another auto or stationary object, soil present on the undercarriage of the vehicle may have been
jarred loose and deposited on the street or sidewalk. It also may be

present on the clothing of a hit-and-run victim. Soil may also be removed from a particular location by a vehicle, usually embedded in the tires or undercarriage.

Weapons and tools used to commit crimes may have been set down momentarily at the scene of a crime and soil may have become embedded on them and, if they are recovered in the possession of the perpetrator, an analysis of the soil could be an important factor in solving the case.

In some situations where the clothing of an unknown deceased is submitted for examination, and there are no cleaning, laundry or other marks of identification, an analysis of the soil present on the shoes or clothing of the victim may give some indication of his occupation or environment, for example, gardener or construction worker.

As would be expected, shoes offer the best surfaces for soil deposits to accumulate. Whereas in many cases only traces of soil are present on clothing, soil in bulk form may have stuck to the soles and heels of the shoes, especially at the juncture of the sole and heel.

When collecting soil, care must be exercised so as not to destroy other trace materials that may be present. For proper analysis, a representative sample of soil should be collected from the scene whenever possible. Samples should be recovered from an area approximately eight to twelve feet in diameter, with samples obtained from every quadrant and placed in separate, clean pillboxes, vials, bottles or other suitable containers. If soil samples are to be taken from a footprint, photographs and casts of the footprint must be completed before any soil is removed from the impression.

The clothing or shoes to be examined for the presence of soil deposits should be submitted to the laboratory for examinations as soon as possible. This is particularly true with shoes. Each step taken by the individual after the initial deposit of soil could result in additional overlay of soil on the original soil, making a soil comparison almost impossible. Each garment and shoe should be placed in separate, sealed plastic bags or other suitable container so that any soil that may fall off during transit may be recovered from the container. When cases involve vehicles, the soil should be recovered at the point of impact if this can be ascertained. During the postmortem examination of a homicide victim, any soil present on the body should be recovered, including any from beneath the fingernails.

The analysis and comparison of soil is important in that it may establish that a particular person or object was at a specific location or that a person or object came in contact with another person or object. But the accurate, scientific comparison of soil is very difficult because of the presence of extremely small particles not capable of accurate analysis.

The analysis and comparison of soil may be accomplished microscopically and with other laboratory instruments. Initially, the heterogeneous mixture is studied through the stereo-binocular microscope and the larger, more easily identified components are removed. Using the polarizing microscope and crystallographic studies, the particles may be identified. The sample is then passed through a series of sieves to determine particle size and distribution. The use of a density gradient (described under glass analysis) serves to furnish information about particle density and as a comparison tool. In addition, the soil may be subjected to spectrographic analysis to determine the chemical elements present in the sample. X-ray diffraction and differential thermal analysis may also be employed in the analytical schema, in addition to qualitative and quantitative chemical analysis.

THE TOOLS OF THE MICROANALYST

In the examination of physical evidence, the microanalyst must, of necessity, be an expert in microscopy. The use of proper optics, illuminators and filters and the correct preparation of specimens for examination are essential if the desired results are to be obtained. In addition, the microanalyst should possess a thorough working knowledge of photomacrography and photomicrography, both in color and black and white. Standards, such as fibers, paints, safe insulation, glass and so on, should be retained in the laboratory reference file for identification and comparison purposes. In addition, the microanalyst must be trained in the manipulation of the smallest of specimens without damaging, altering or losing the specimen.

Perhaps the most important and most used microscope in the examination of physical evidence is the stereo-binocular microscope. In the hands of the trained microanalyst, this instrument affords a magnified image of the object exactly as it appears in nature, the three dimensions of length, breadth and depth being visible. It is employed in the examination of bulk items such as clothing and weapons and also minute items such as glass, hairs, fibers, paint, soil and other trace materials. One of the best uses for the instrument is to extract and isolate minute particles that may be present on a larger item and to separate debris into separate constituents (see Figure 52A).

A second important instrument at the disposal of the trained microanalyst is the polarizing (petrographic) microscope. The unit allows for the study of specimens in very exact detail with respect to their physical and chemical properties. The assignment of mathematical values to the results of these examinations and tests makes this instrument extremely valuable. It is used to identify and compare hair, fibers, glass, paint, soil, dust, safe insulation and other trace materials (see Figure 52B).

The comparison microscope is another widely used and valuable instrument to the microanalyst. It actually consists of two microscopes with identical optical systems, matched objectives and eyepieces, and identical light sources of equal intensity. The two microscopes are connected by an optical bridge. One specimen is placed on the stage of one microscope, and a second specimen is placed on the other microscope stage (see Figure 52C). When these specimens are observed through the optical bridge they appear to be side by side as if both specimens were in one field (one specimen appearing as a continuation of the other), as was earlier illustrated in Figure 45. This instrument is used mainly in the comparison of

Figure 52. In A, a technician is using a stereo-binocular microscope equipped with a 35 mm camera to locate, photograph and remove paint particles embedded in a garment. B illustrates a polarizing microscope with hot-stage attachment for determining melting points and refractive index and for examining crystals, hair, fibers, soil and debris. C shows a comparison microscope, used for the study of evidence by transmitted light.

morphological characteristics. It is extremely valuable in the comparison of hairs and fibers.

The phase, interference and dark-field microscopes are also available to the microanalyst. These instruments, through the use of special objectives, condensers and illuminators, refract certain rays of light coming through the objective, improving the resolving power of the microscope and thereby exhibiting in greater detail the object being examined. The use of these instruments is usually resorted to in the examinations of certain types of specimens or to search for characteristics that will not be revealed in great detail by the ordinary bright-field microscope.

Other instruments, such as the ordinary compound microscope, are also used for routine examinations not requiring a great degree of sophisticated optics.

Accessory optics, illuminators and filters are combined with the foregoing units to provide the trained microanalyst with the necessary resolution, magnification and contrast control needed for the examination, identification and comparison of specimens submitted to him for analysis. In addition, photomacrographs and photomicrographs may be taken of the specimens for a permanent record and for court presentation.

Of equal importance to the microanalyst is the use of such instrumentation as emission spectrography, infrared and ultraviolet spectrophotometry, X-ray diffraction and gas chromatography. These instruments, used in conjunction with microscopic examinations of physical evidence, provide the analyst with the necessary equipment for the examination of physical evidence. In addition, the microanalyst should have available to him such sophisticated instrumentation as that needed to use neutron activation analysis techniques, the scanning electron microscope and atomic absorption.

THE FIELD INVESTIGATOR'S COOPERATION

The field investigator must bear in mind that any information the microanalyst can extract from the physical evidence submitted for examination depends for its value on the manner in which the physical evidence is recovered, packaged and transported to the laboratory. In addition to the evidence, a report should be submitted to the laboratory with all pertinent facts relating to the incident as known by the field investigator so as to acquaint the laboratory examiners with facts that may suggest to them particular tests and examinations which may speed up the flow of information back to the field investigator.

When submitting physical evidence to the laboratory, each container (pillbox, vial, bottle, test tube, envelope, box, plastic bag, etc.) should be tagged or labeled with the following information:

1. Contents
2. Owner or possessor, if known
3. Location where evidence recovered
4. Date and time evidence was recovered
5. Type of crime
6. Name of victim
7. Case number, if assigned
8. Initials of person who found and recovered evidence

To prevent loss, alteration or contamination of physical evidence, the following should be done by the field investigator:

1. Avoid handling of the evidence by too many people
2. Avoid cutting, tearing or ripping clothing
3. Place each item or sample of evidence in a separate container
4. Do not attempt to separate evidence found together
5. Do not apply fingerprint powder on blood in searching for latent fingerprints. Submit the entire article to the laboratory. If unable to submit entire article, request laboratory assistance
6. Gather any possibly pertinent evidence in sufficient quantity. In some instances a return to the scene will find the blood washed away, debris removed, surfaces repainted and glass replaced.

If evidence is properly handled and promptly submitted to the laboratory, stains, hairs, fibers and trace materials can be examined by a qualified microanalyst.

The opinions and conclusions of a qualified microanalyst are readily admitted in evidence when the exhibits involved have met the required tests of authenticity.

Chapter 7

Biological Evidence

At any crime scene, but primarily at scenes of homicides, sex offenses and burglaries, traces of bodily substances from either the victim or the offender may be discovered. The examination of these
traces by the trained specialist can reveal much useful information
for the investigators and can also frequently yield evidence that
may be presented in court. Among the most frequently encountered
traces of biological evidence are blood, semen, saliva, fecal matter
and perspiration. Another area of biological evidence, usually handled by specialists in a department different from that dealing with
the above items of trace evidence, consists of blood-alcohol tests to
determine the degree of intoxication. Because the latter also involves a study of blood, its discussion is included in this chapter.

BLOOD

In any case where blood is found at a crime scene, or on a
weapon, clothing or any item that the field investigator believes is
or could be associated with a crime, routine serological testing by
laboratory personnel should be performed. When the field investigator is not certain that stains discovered at a crime scene or on an
item are blood, the traces should also be submitted to the serologist
for examination. Many times stains that appeared to be rust to the
field investigator subsequently turn out to be human blood stains
after analysis by competent laboratory personnel.

Blood is usually recovered as (1) fresh blood, (2) clotted blood, (3)
smears or (4) blood flakes. The general rule for the field investigator

to remember is to submit the entire bloodstained item to the laboratory, whenever possible. This is particularly true when weapons are involved or when the bloodstained clothing of a suspect is recovered.

In the case of clothing, wet blood present thereon may be removed and placed in a vial or bottle and the garment allowed to dry. The garment is then placed in a plastic bag and submitted to the laboratory, along with the wet specimen. If several items of clothing are involved, each should be placed in a separate plastic bag.

No effort should be made to examine an item for latent fingerprints, which would necessitate superimposing fingerprint powders over blood. The fingerprint powders may interfere with subsequent serological tests, particularly in determining the blood group of the stain. In some cases, as for example when blood is found on a wall, it would be impossible to submit the entire item to the laboratory for analysis. When this happens the bloodstain may be removed and placed in a clean container. Prior to removing the blood, however, the stains should be photographed. The blood distribution patterns on any item may furnish valuable information. For example, the presence of splatters (splashes) of blood at a certain location may indicate the actual scene of an assault even though the victim's body was found at a different location. Blood splatters may furnish other information to trained examiners as well, such as the height or distance from the source of blood to the point where the stains are discovered.

Collecting Blood Traces

To recover a specimen of fluid blood, a clean medicine dropper can be used to siphon blood from the surface. The blood is then placed in a clean vial, and the vial sealed to prevent loss or contamination. Dried bloodstains may be recovered by using several cotton swabs moistened with distilled water; the cotton swabs are dipped onto the blood until the swabs become a reddish-brown color. The swabs are then placed in a clean vial or bottle, and the container sealed.

Dried flakes of suspected blood can be scraped onto a clean piece of paper by using a clean knife, razor blade or tongue depressor. The flakes and the paper are placed in a clean pillbox, which is then sealed. Each container must be suitably marked, and when suspected stains are recovered from different locations each specimen should be placed in a separate container. The specimens, wet or dry, should be submitted to the laboratory as quickly as possible, especially during warm weather. Heat, humidity and sunlight have a negative effect on blood, and blood decomposes in a short time without proper preservatives.

The examination of blood specimens seeks answers to the following questions:

1. Is the stain blood?
2. If it is blood, is it of animal or human origin?
3. If it is human blood, what is the blood grouping?
4. If animal, what species of animal?

Visual and microscopic observations in addition to chemical and serological tests and instrumental analysis are methods employed in the examination of blood specimens.

Before discussing the various tests and analyses of blood specimens, one point must be made perfectly clear. Blood as evidence is what is referred to as a "negative-positive"! No statement can be made that two blood samples are identical, but the serologist can state at times that two blood specimens are not identical. For example, if the blood on the clothing of a suspect is of group A and the blood group of the victim is also group A, the only positive statement that the serologist can validly make is that both bloods are of the same blood group. He cannot state that the two specimens came from the same origin. If the blood on the clothing of a suspect is of group B and the victim's blood group is A, the serologist may then state that the blood on the suspect's clothing could not have come from the victim. This statement applies not only to blood groups but also to other constituents, such as albumins, globulins and enzymes, which are present in blood.

Preliminary Tests for Blood

One of the most widely used preliminary tests for blood is the benzidine test. Many field investigators resort to this test to determine if a particular stain could be blood. The test is not specific for blood, and a positive reaction indicates only that the substance may be blood. Further laboratory testing is required to establish whether or not the substance is blood and to classify the blood as to species—animal or human.

The benzidine test is simple and based on the presence of hemoglobin in blood. Peroxidase, an enzyme found in the blood, speeds up the oxidation of benzidine with the formation of a blue color. A saturated solution of benzidine in acetic acid is made up and placed in a brown bottle (brown glass prevents decomposition of the reagent). A second reagent bottle contains hydrogen peroxide. The stain may be tested directly, but it is best to remove some of the stain on a cotton swab and add one or two drops of the benzidine reagent. At this point there should be no color change. On adding one or two drops of hydrogen peroxide, a blue-green color should appear if hemoglobin is present.

The various steps in the course of a benzidine test are illustrated in Figure 53. When confronted with a suspected bloodstain on a knife, the stain is removed with a cotton swab that has been moistened with distilled water (Figure 53A); then the benzidine reagent is applied to the suspected stain (53B). A color change occurs when hydrogen peroxide is placed on a cotton swab that contains blood (53C).

It must be remembered that interfering agents such as vegetable peroxidase, chemical oxidants or contamination may give a false positive reaction. In any event, the suspected stain should be submitted to a serologist for the necessary confirmatory tests.

In addition to the benzidine test there are other preliminary chemical tests for blood. Some of these are the phenolphthalein (color) test, the guaiacum (color) test and the Teichmann (crystal) test. Again, none of these tests is specific for blood, and confirmatory tests are necessary.

Species Origin of Blood

The confirmatory test for identifying a substance as blood, and further classifying it as being of animal or human origin, is the precipitin test. It is specific for blood and identifies the proteins present in blood. The test is based on the ability of an animal, usually a rabbit, injected with human blood, to reject the human serum by building up a precipitin (antibody). The precipitins developed by the animal react with the proteins of human blood serum to form a white cloudy precipitate. This precipitin (antihuman serum) will not react with proteins from another animal. Suitable controls consisting of known human blood and animal blood are tested concurrently with the suspected blood to ensure the accuracy and specificity of the antiserum. In the same manner, antiserum can be

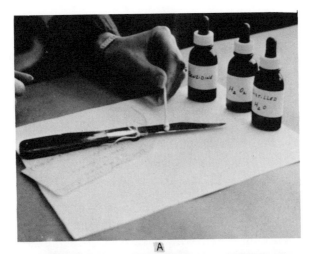

A

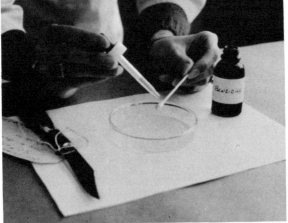

B

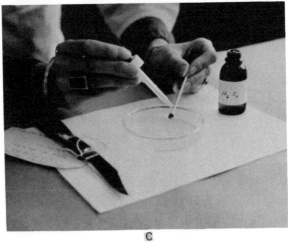

C

Figure 53.

prepared specifically for a particular animal species (dog, horse) when the blood is of animal origin and it is necessary to determine the animal's species.

In addition to the above test, the precipitin test may also be performed by the Agar Double Diffusion method. Agar (an extract of sea weed) is layered onto a glass slide approximately 3 x 3 inches. A series of small holes are made in the agar around a center well. The antihuman serum along with the suitable controls are placed in the outer holes. The extract from the suspected stain is placed in the center well. The technique relies on the diffusion of the antigen in the stain toward the antibody (antihuman serum) in the agar. Where both diffusing fronts meet, a white precipitation line appears in the agar, indicating positive results.

Blood Grouping

After determining that the blood is of human origin, the blood is further classified as to blood group. Blood group determination is based on antigen-antibody reactions. For example, let us examine the ABO system. In 1900 Landsteiner established that the serum of one individual would clump (agglutinate) the red blood cells of another individual. The explanation for this was that the red blood cells contain a substance known as an antigen and the serum of the blood contains antibodies. The two antigens in the ABO blood system are the antigens A and B and the two antibodies in the ABO system are anti-A (alpha) and anti-B (beta). In the blood of a human being, either the A antigen or the B antigen, both A and B antigens, or neither A nor B antigen is present in the red blood cells.

These antigens may also be referred to as blood-group factors; therefore, a person having A antigen in his red blood cells has group-A blood, a person having B antigen has group-B blood, a person having both A and B antigens has group-AB blood, and a person who has neither A nor B antigens in his red blood cells has group-O blood. If a person has an A antigen in his red blood cells he cannot have an anti-A antibody in his serum, for this would clump his own cells. The same is true of an individual having B antigen in his blood cells: he cannot have anti-B antibody in his serum. It follows that a person with both A and B antigens in his blood cells can have neither anti-A nor anti-B antibodies in his serum. However, a person who has neither antigen A nor antigen B in his red blood cells (group O) has both antibodies, anti-A and anti-B, in his serum.

As stated before, the determination of blood groups is based on the clumping of the red cells, or the reaction of an antigen with an antibody. Therefore the following is true. A person with A antigen in his blood can have his red cells clumped, or agglutinated, by a person having the antibody anti-A in his serum, which could only be a person of blood group B or O. A person with B antigen in his blood can have his red cells agglutinated by a person having the antibody anti-B in his serum, which could only be a person of blood group A or O. A person having the antigens A and B in his blood can have his blood agglutinated by a person having the antibody anti-A or anti-B or both anti-A and anti-B in his serum, which could be a person of group A, B or O. A person having neither antigen A nor antigen B in his blood (group O) cannot have his red blood cells agglutinated. With specific serums, anti-A and anti-B, it is possible to determine the blood group of any blood in the ABO system accurately. Blood of group A will be agglutinated by anti-A serum; blood of group B will be agglutinated by anti-B serum; AB blood will be agglutinated by both anti-A and anti-B serum; and blood of group O will not be agglutinated by either anti-A or anti-B serum.

When fresh liquid blood is submitted to the laboratory for analysis, the specimen should be grouped in the ABO, MN and Rh systems. The principles involved in the MN and Rh systems are the same as those of the ABO system—the detection of specific blood-group factors by the agglutination of red cells by specific antiserums. When dried bloodstains no longer containing red blood cells are submitted for blood-group determination, the procedure is again based on antibody-antigen reaction, but the technique is somewhat more complicated and requires some expertise. The absorption-elution and the mixed agglutination tests are most frequently used to determine the blood groups of dried stains. Both of these methods rely on the ability of the antigen present in the bloodstained material to absorb its specific antiserum. Again, in the ABO system, if the bloodstain contains antigen A, anti-A serum will be absorbed by the stain; if the stain contains antigen B, anti-B serum will be absorbed; if the stain contains both antigens A and B, both serum anti-A and anti-B will be absorbed by the stain. If the stain contains neither A nor B antigen, neither anti-A nor anti-B serum will be absorbed. The blood group can then be determined by eluting (liberating) the absorbed serum, if any, and testing the same against known A, B and O red blood cells, as is done in blood-grouping fresh liquid blood containing red blood cells. Suitable controls must be incorporated to ensure accuracy.

Other blood-grouping techniques such as the Lattes or crust method and the absorption-inhibition test may also be used, but they lack the success enjoyed by the absorption-elution technique, especially when small amounts of specimen are involved.

Other constituents present in the blood may also be identified by a process known as electrophoresis. These plasma proteins consist of albumins and globulins, with the globulins containing other proteins known as haptoglobins. The proteins are present in blood in different forms. In addition to the plasma proteins, many enzymes are also present in different forms in the blood and may be identified through electrophoresis.

In electrophoresis, the blood is placed in a well in a layer of agar on a glass plate. Voltage is introduced, causing the protein molecules that carry different electrical charges to separate from the blood and migrate across the agar. Suitable dyes are then applied to the gel after migration has been completed and the resulting pattern of separated proteins serves to identify the proteins that were present in the blood. Other proteins may require an antiserum that is specific for particular proteins, in which case the same procedure is followed but a trough is cut into the gel parallel to the direction of migration and the specific antiserum is added in the trough after the separation of the blood proteins. The antiserum diffuses from the trough and reacts with the serum proteins that have separated along a curved line in the gel. The resulting pattern is then interpreted in order to identify the proteins present. The use of antiserums to identify serum proteins that have been separated by voltage in a gel is known as immuno-electrophoresis. Enzymes present in blood may also be separated by electrophoresis and identified; the process involves a chemical reaction that results in a colored compound induced by the enzyme.

Blood-group substances are present not only in blood. Approximately 80–85% of the population, known as secretors, have blood-group substances in their saliva, tears, perspiration, semen, gastric contents and so forth. The quantity of blood-group antigens in semen and saliva, for example, is much greater than that found in red blood cells, so that the blood groups of semen and saliva may be determined from a small amount of specimen. The remaining portion of the population does not secrete these blood-group substances.

SEMEN

Semen is usually associated with cases involving rape, but it may also be recovered from the body or clothing of a homicide victim or may even be found at the scene of a burglary.

When clothing is recovered with suspected seminal stains, each garment should be placed in a separate plastic bag. Care must be taken to avoid exposing the suspected stain to friction and the garment should not be folded at the area of the stain. This may be accomplished by attaching the garment bearing the suspected stain to a sheet of cardboard prior to placing the garment in the plastic bag.

In homicide cases in which a female is the victim, oral, vaginal and rectal smears or swabs should be obtained through the medical examiner and examined for the presence of semen. This may establish that the slaying was sexually motivated. And when the victim or the perpetrator of a homicide is suspected of being a homosexual, oral and rectal swabs should be obtained and examined for the presence of semen.

The identification of semen plays a very important role in establishing whether or not a sexual assault has occurred. Finding semen in an auto, on bed clothing or on the clothing of the victim may corroborate a victim's allegation of rape. In every case in which the victim alleges sexual assault, he or she should be examined by a physician and swabs or smears taken from the bodily orifices.

Semen is the product of the male reproductive organs, consisting of spermatozoa together with secretions of various glands (the prostate gland in man and other mammals). Fresh liquid semen has an alkaline odor that is readily detectable. Dried semen stains appear as mucous crystalline incrustations that are grayish white. Semen contains spermatozoa in the ratio of approximately 100,000,000 spermatozoa per ml of semen. The normal, healthy male ejaculates approximately 3.5 ml of semen, containing about 350,000,000 spermatozoa. The principal parts of a spermatozoon are the head, neck, body and tail. It measures approximately .05 mm or $1/500$ of an inch in length and appears oval in a flat view and pear shaped in profile.

The most specific test for the presence of semen consists of the isolation and identification of spermatozoa. Figure 54 illustrates how evidence of semen may be preserved for presentation in court. In 54A the mucous crystalline deposits on the garment are clearly visible. 54B shows a photomicrograph of spermatozoa extracted from the garment. 54C illustrates the proper method of preserving and marking evidence for future identification. In illustration 54B, an aqueous extract of the suspected stain was made and placed on a microscope slide. It was then fixed and stained with a Carbol-Eosin-Fuchsin stain to which a small amount of Methylene Blue had been added. The specimen was then examined microscopically at 430-magnification utilizing phase optics.

In many instances, microscopic examinations of extracts of seminal deposits may not reveal the presence of spermatozoa, which may be the result of conditions known as oligospermia and azoospermia, in which the semen contains only a few or no spermatozoa. When this occurs it is necessary to use other methods to identify semen.

The acid phosphatase test is used extensively in forensic laboratories. Research has established that semen has a high acid phosphatase activity compared to that of other bodily fluids. An extract of the suspected stain is treated with a properly prepared solution of phenolic phosphate ester. If acid phosphatase is present, the phenolic phosphate ester will be hydrolyzed to phosphate ion and phenol. The phenol then reacts with another substance to form a colored product indicative of the presence of semen. Although this test strongly indicates the presence of semen, certain vegetable juices and contraceptive gels may give false positive reactions. Again, the reaction must occur within a specified time and the color obtained must be of a specific concentration.

Semen may also be identified immunologically through the use of the Agar Double Diffusion technique, described earlier as a method for establishing the species origin of blood. The test involves the use of an antihuman serum that can be prepared by injecting an animal with human semen. The resulting serum contains antibodies specific for proteins in human semen. Other methods for the identification of semen include paper and thin-layer chromatography and the Brentamine Fast Blue test.

A

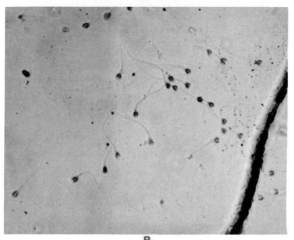

B

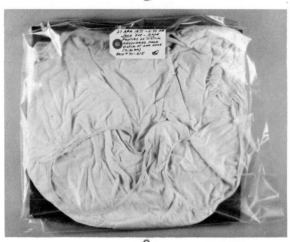

C

Figure 54.

OTHER BIOLOGICAL EVIDENCE

SALIVA. The identification of saliva stains may be important in the investigation of criminal incidents. For example, a cigarette or handkerchief left behind at a crime scene may have saliva stains on it. If the person responsible for the stains is a "secretor" (see before on page 121), it may be possible to identify his blood group. This is also true of saliva stains on postage stamps and on the glued portion of envelopes, for instance.

FECAL MATTER. The identification of fecal deposits on clothing occurs frequently in cases involving homosexuality or homosexual assaults, but deposits of fecal matter may also be present at crime scenes because of an abnormal mental aberration of the perpetrator or simply because of nervous tension or necessity. The possibility that the blood group may be determined from the feces, thus aiding in tracing the criminal, should not be overlooked. Also, a microscopic examination of fecal matter may reveal the presence of a particular type of parasite, which may indicate that the perpetrator suffers from a specific malady.

VOMITUS. Vomitus present on a garment at a particular area may corroborate the story of a victim of a deviate sexual assault. Blood group determination is again possible, thus aiding in locating the criminal or eliminating suspects who are excluded by the test results.

PERSPIRATION. As with other biological evidence, perspiration stains may be important in tracing a criminal through the blood group of the stain. A criminal often leaves garments at the scene of his activity, and most shirts and coats have perspiration stains at the armpits. This also applies to any headgear that the criminal might have taken off and then forgotten or lost in running away from the scene or from the police. The sweatband on the interior of the hat is an excellent source of perspiration stains.

Perspiration stains, fecal matter, vomitus, saliva and other bodily fluids may also be important evidence in cases involving crimes such as abortion and infanticide in which clothing, towels, bedding and the like are involved or used.

Blood-Alcohol Tests for Intoxication

The impact alcohol consumption has had upon traffic safety need not be emphasized. Gruesome statistics are quoted by the communications media whenever a holiday pours millions of "occasional" driver-drinkers onto the highways. Since driving while under the influence of intoxicating beverages is an offense in all states, the detection of the degree of intoxication becomes an important part of the modern crime laboratory functions if convictions are to be obtained. This is particularly true since the standard tests for "driving under the influence of alcohol" given by investigators (coordination, balancing, walking and turning, finger-to-nose, picking up coins, speech and pupil tests) have not been very effective in obtaining convictions.

The degree of intoxication cannot be accurately measured by the amount of liquor a person has consumed, but it can be determined to a reliable extent by measuring the quantity of the alcohol in the beverages which has reached his brain. It is the alcohol content of the brain that directly causes most of the physical and psychological effects attributable to the presence of alcohol in the body.

There is no such thing as normal alcohol in bodily substances. When alcohol is taken into the somach, it is not digested. Approximately ten to twenty percent is absorbed into the bloodstream through the stomach wall. The remainder is absorbed in the small intestines. In normal consumption of liquor, the alcohol is absorbed in the bloodstream in approximately 45 to 90 minutes after consumption. The rate of absorption is affected by the quantity and alcohol content of the beverage consumed, by the amount of food or liquid in the stomach, and by the nature of the food in the stomach. Fatty foods and sugars appear to retard absorption slightly.

The absorbed alcohol does not change. It remains alcohol. Once absorbed into the bloodstream, the alcohol is distributed throughout the body according to the amount of water in the various tissues. Very little will be found in the bones or in fatty tissue, whereas substantial amounts will be found in the blood plasma and in watery tissue such as the brain and nervous system. Some of the alcohol will be found in fluids such as sweat, spinal fluid, saliva, tears and urine. The presence of alcohol in the bodily fluids can be determined by chemical tests.

The most reliable chemical test for intoxication is a direct analysis of the brain tissue, but its use is obviously confined to corpses, before decay and putrefaction. So is the analysis of spinal fluid. The other tests that are suitable for use on living persons are limited to analyses of the blood, breath and urine.

Blood Analysis for Intoxication

Of the practical methods for determining the alcohol content of a body, a direct analysis of the blood is considered the most reliable. The main limitations to this testing method are the necessity of having a doctor or qualified technician obtain the sample under sterile conditions, the evidentiary requirement of preserving the chain of evidence, and the fact that many people are hesitant to consent to having a needle stuck in their veins. Because of these and other limitations, blood analysis as a test for intoxication has not been as widely used in the United States as some of the other chemical tests.

Breath Analysis for Intoxication

The so-called "breath tests" for intoxication are based on the assumption that the breath sample collected in a balloon or other apparatus is saturated with alcohol vapor at the temperature of the normal respiratory tract. A number of instruments have been developed over the years to assist in the making of a breath analysis for blood-alcohol content. The first one was the Drunkometer, developed in 1931 by Dr. R. N. Harger at Indiana University Medical School. Others have been the Alcometer, the Intoximeter, the Breathalyzer, the Photo-Electric Intoximeter, the D.P.C. Intoximeter, the Breathtester and the Kitagawa-Wringt apparatus, to name only the best known. Of them, the Drunkometer, the Intoximeter and the Breathalyzer are the most widely used. All operate on the same principles that were established by Dr. Harger in 1931.

The Drunkometer works on the principle of the decolorization of a measured quantity of permanganate by the alcohol present in the breath, captured in a rubber balloon. The concentration of alcohol is determined from the amount of breath required to cause the chemical reaction evidenced by the discoloration. The final step of the process involves a mathematical conversion from the Drunkometer reading to the blood-alcohol percentage.

The Intoximeter, developed by Dr. G. C. Forrester, utilizes magnesium perchlorate instead of the permanganate used in the Drunk-ometer. This test has a drawback in that it requires testimony concerning the original condition of the apparatus and the changes caused by the test, thus requiring the attendance of an expert at the place where the test is taken. The Drunkometer, on the other hand, can be operated by a police officer who has had a short period of training in the operation of the equipment.

The Breathalyzer, developed by Captain R. F. Borkenstein of the Indiana State Police, operates on the principle that when breath is passed through a solution of liquid sulfuric acid and potassium di-chromate the normal yellow color of the solution turns green if al-cohol is present.

Because of the variety of instruments and the many pitfalls inher-ent in all of the techniques which must be avoided to obtain evidence that will be admissible in court, police officers need spe-cial training in conducting the tests and interpreting the results. Most manufacturers provide training for law enforcement officers in those areas in which special police school instruction is not avail-able.

Urinalysis for Intoxication

The analysis of urine suffers from some serious drawbacks. The relationship between the alcohol concentration in urine and that in the blood is rather complicated; since it takes time for a quantity of urine to collect in the bladder, the higher concentration of alcohol occurs at a later time in urine than in blood. Except for a short peak period, the alcohol concentration in blood changes constantly, either rising or falling; in urine, the changes do not follow the same pattern as with blood. For these reasons, urinalysis is not nearly as widely used as the tests already discussed. It requires the use of a sophisticated laboratory for analysis and is encumbered by additional factors. The results may be affected by the bladder con-dition before or after the consumption of alcohol. If alcohol is con-sumed with a full bladder, the tests will inaccurately underestimate the degree of blood-alcohol content. Conversely, if an individual consumes alcohol with an empty bladder some time prior to the test and does not void himself, the results can easily overestimate the amount of alcohol in the blood at the time of the test. Alcohol in the bladder is not an active agent in causing symptoms of intoxication, and, like the test for estimating the amount of alcohol ingested, it is not as reliable an index for determining the degree of intoxication. Two specimens taken at thirty-minute intervals would augment the reliability of the urine test.

Chapter 8

Neutron Activation Analysis

In order to keep pace with the ever increasing crime rate and the great mobility of criminals, the police have turned to more and more sophisticated methods for proving criminal guilt. One recent development, an offshoot of post World War II nuclear technology, is called neutron activation analysis, commonly referred to as NAA. This new technique for the identification and comparison of physical evidence has wide application and potential usefulness in the field of criminalistics because it provides a most significant method for the nondestructive analysis of innumerable types of physical evidence. Because of the requirement for special facilities and highly skilled technicians to operate the equipment, NAA has not been used extensively at the local law enforcement levels, although the federal government, some state crime laboratories and a few large metropolitan police departments are using it more and more.

Neutron activation analysis is a nuclear, as opposed to a chemical or spectrographic, method of quantitatively analyzing samples for the elements they contain. The process can be briefly described as follows: a sample to be analyzed is first irradiated or bombarded ("activated") with nuclear particles, usually an intense stream of neutrons. Through nuclear reaction with the nuclei of the irradiated atoms, the neutrons make most of the elements of the sample radioactive. They disintegrate with the emission of high-energy electromagnetic radiations called gamma rays. The gamma rays are then counted ("analyzed"), a process which reveals the half-lives of the radioactive nuclei and their gamma ray energies. It also permits the detection, identification and quantitative measurement of the ele-

ments by comparison with the data obtained from known substances. How this works is illustrated in Figure 55.

In many cases the activated sample can be counted without
being destroyed, that is, without chemical treatment. If the neutron
flux available is extremely high, as it is in a nuclear reactor, NAA
becomes an extremely sensitive method of analysis. In fact, for the
majority of known elements it is the most sensitive method of analysis known (a typical element can be detected down to levels as low
as one-billionth of a gram). The method, when properly used, is so
accurate that it is said to be 99.99% reliable.

Research in the field was originally sponsored by the U.S. Atomic
Energy Commission. One of the pioneer scientists was Dr. Vincent
P. Guinn, manager and technical director of the Activation Analysis
Department at Gulf General Atomic in San Diego. Other pioneers
in the field include Howard L. Schlesinger, of the Internal Revenue
Service, who was the expert witness in the first two trials in which
NAA test results were admitted; Maynard J. Pro, also of the Inter-
nal Revenue Service; and Donald E. Bryan, of Gulf General
Atomic. All have been frequent expert witnesses for the prosecution.
NAA evidence has been admitted in trials in connection with the
examination of soils, automobile putty, adhesive tape, paints, organic and inorganic particles, grease, bullets, gun metal, galvanized
wire, pipe joint compound, safe insulation, moonshine, gunshot residues, wheat paste, rope, heroin and marijuana.

THE METHOD

First, as is the case with all trace evidence, the unknown material
and the matter with which it is to be compared must be gathered
and transmitted to the appropriate testing place. After contami-
nants have been removed, the samples, along with control items to
detect whether processing has added impurities, are placed in vials.
These vials are then introduced into the reactor by means of a
pneumatically operated "rabbit tube" and are placed on a rotary
rack inside the reactor. This is done to introduce all of the sample
at about the same time. The rotary rack is used so that the neutron
flux density—that is, the number of bombarding neutrons per
square centimeter per second—is the same for all the sample, and to
avoid irradiating one sample more than another. After spending an
appropriate time in the reactor, the samples are removed. This time

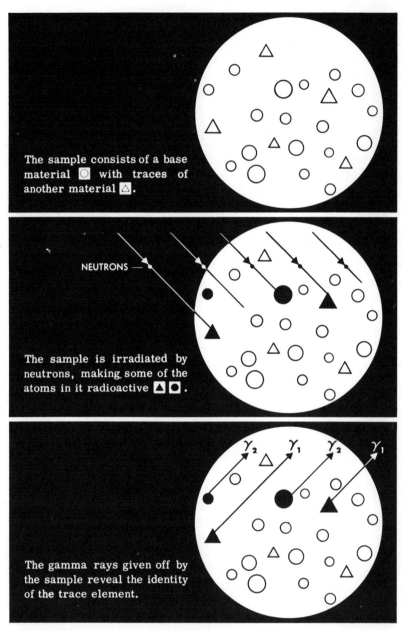

The sample consists of a base material 〇 with traces of another material △.

NEUTRONS

The sample is irradiated by neutrons, making some of the atoms in it radioactive ▲ ●.

γ_2 γ_1 γ_2 γ_1

The gamma rays given off by the sample reveal the identity of the trace element.

Figure 55. In neutron activation analysis, traces of various elements can be identified and measured by analyzing the gamma rays they give off after being irradiated with neutrons or other nuclear particles. Courtesy: U.S. Atomic Energy Commission.

period of irradiation varies from one to several hours, depending on the elements to be identified.

After the removal from the reactor, the samples are "counted," which is done by placing the sample in a scintillation crystal. The unique properties of this crystal cause it to give off a flash of light when struck by a gamma ray. The intensity of the flash of light is in proportion to the energy of the gamma ray. Since each isotope emits gamma rays of distinct energy levels, the brightness of the flash of light shows the presence of certain elements.

The flashes of light, in turn, are detected by photomultiplier tubes, which convert the light energy into electrical pulses in proportion to the brightness of the flash. These electrical pulses are then fed into a differential analyzer, which counts the number of flashes of light for each energy level or "channel." These results are then plotted graphically on an oscilloscope, or are stored on tape for later display. (See Figure 56.) Additional techniques such as spectrum stripping and heavier irradiation are used to detect the presence of more elements.

Some of the earliest applications of NAA as an evidentiary tool were in soil comparisons to show that mud from a truck carrying moonshine was the same mud found at the site of the still and that the truck had been at that still. Other court cases that featured NAA evidence dealt with the identification of the same trace elements in moonshine and spring water near a still and with the identification of narcotics to show a common source. Hair has also been analyzed not only to show that a particular strand probably came from a particular person's head but also to indicate the presence of trace elements such as arsenic in the hair.

NAA Test for Gunshot Residues

Gulf General Atomic has developed a method for detecting gunshot residues on the gun hand of a person who has recently fired a revolver or automatic pistol or even, in some instances, rifles and shotguns. The NAA test is far more accurate than the ordinary diphenylamine (paraffin) test. The method involves the removal of any possible gunshot residues from a selected area on the back of the suspect's hand by a modified paraffin procedure that uses a thin layer of selected paraffin and no gauze. The paraffin lift is then activated in the nuclear reactor, which produces a radiochemical sepa-

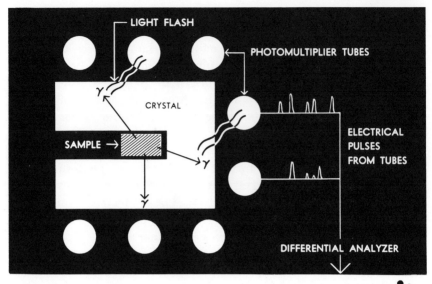

Figure 56. Diagram of how an activated sample is counted. The lower portion of the diagram represents a pictorial image of what is seen on the screen of an oscilloscope. Courtesy: Gulf General Atomic

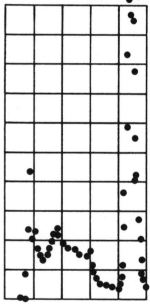

ration of any radioactive barium and antimony thus produced. A quantitative measurement of the amounts of these two now radioactive elements by the appropriate counting methods completes the process.

These two elements are present in the primers used in U.S. and many foreign made ammunitions. The amounts of them deposited in even a single firing are normally much larger than the bare traces of these elements that may be present on the hands of persons who have not recently fired a gun.

Because of the high cost of the equipment involved, it is unlikely that many law enforcement agencies will be able to acquire the necessary installation. As a result, Gulf General Atomic instituted in 1968 a forensic activation analysis service on a nonprofit basis for the assistance of law enforcement agencies. At that time, the cost of the services was publicized as follows:

1. Nondestructive comparison of two evidence samples (such as paint, glass, metal, plastic, rubber, paper, grease, rope, tape, soil, marijuana, etc., but excluding hair): $160. Additional samples of the same type, compared at the same time: $30 per sample.
2. Nondestructive comparison of two strands (or samples) of hair: $250. Additional hair samples to be compared at the same time: $50 per sample.
3. Analysis of one gunshot-paraffin lift: $190. Additional paraffin-lift samples analyzed at the same time: $40 per sample. Special paraffin removal kits that require a standard procedure developed by the company are furnished and must be used.

The radiochemist who performs the tests is available to testify as an expert witness at cost.

While NAA testimony has been admitted in some 75 trials between 1964 and 1970, only a few appellate decisions have dealt with it. In the first case, a 1969 New Hampshire Supreme Court decision held that NAA evidence of particles found on the defendant was properly admitted, and that evidence of a similar examination of pubic hair was properly excluded because of lack of specificity. The other cases decided since then have suggested that, because of the reliability and specificity of NAA as a tool for the analysis of trace elements, evidence related to such tests may be admitted.

Although NAA is another valuable diagnostic tool in the hands of a forensic scientist, it is not, or course, a panacea for all of the investigator's difficulties. Its full value has not been sufficiently assessed and much more research is required.

Chapter 9

Spectrographic Voice Identification

Although evidence of the identification of individuals by the sounds of their voices has long been accepted by the courts, the reliability of such identifications is often seriously questioned. Some research has indicated that it is considerably less reliable even than eye witness identifications. In the last decade, however, a new technique of spectrographic voice recognition was developed by Lawrence G. Kersta, formerly with the acoustics and speech research laboratory of the Bell Telephone Laboratories at Murray Hill, New Jersey, which holds some promise of greatly improved accuracy, but it requires a recording not only of the suspect's voice but also of the offender's voice.

Kersta left the Bell System and founded his own company, Voiceprint Laboratories. A means of positively identifying individuals by their voices, relying on scientific instrumentation rather than the human senses, would certainly be a most potent weapon in the arsenal of the law enforcement crime laboratory. Preliminary research and experimentation seem to indicate that we may have available such a voice identification method by the use of the sound spectrograph.

SOUND, SPEECH AND THE VOICE SPECTROGRAPH

Stripped of its complexities, sound can be described as energy in the form of waves or pulses, caused by vibrations. In the speech process, the initial wave producing vibrations is that of the vocal cords. Each vibration causes a compression and corresponding rare-

136

faction of the air, which is the wave or pulse. The time interval between each pulse is called the frequency of the sound and is expressed in cycles per second, abbreviated as cps. It is this frequency
which determines the pitch of the sound. The higher the frequency,
the higher the pitch, and vice versa.

Another characteristic of sound is intensity. In speech this is the
characteristic of loudness. Intensity or loudness is a function of the
amount of energy in the sound wave or pulse. To understand the
difference between frequency and intensity, imagine a gong that is
being struck with a hammer. The force with which the gong is
struck is the intensity; it determines the loudness of the sound produced. The harder the strike, the louder the sound. The frequency,
on the other hand, consists of the speed with which the sound that
is produced vibrates; it determines the pitch of the sound. The
pitch of the sound will remain the same no matter how hard the
gong is struck.

The human voice is capable of a wide range of pitches and intensities. But that is not the only thing that makes it different from
the gong. The human voice is incapable of producing only one
pitch or frequency at a time. Instead, all speech is composed of several frequencies produced simultaneously. The lowest pitch or frequency is called the "fundamental" and is accompanied by several
different tones called "overtones," each having frequencies which
are even multiples of the fundamental. It is these overtones that
give the voice its tonal quality.

The frequency at which air particles vibrate, which is the same as
the frequency of the sound source, is called the frequency of the
sound wave. If that frequency falls between roughly 20 cps and
20,000 cps, the air vibration can be perceived by the human ear as
"sound." There exist sound waves at much higher frequencies, but
our human hearing system is not adapted to perceive them; they
are inaudible to man. Not all creatures hear within the same frequency ranges as do human beings. Everyone is familiar, for example, with the "silent" dog whistles. The whistle emits a sound of a
frequency that human ears cannot detect, though the hearing
mechanism of the dog is equipped to receive it. Another example is
bats, who use very high frequency sound waves to locate their prey,
much as we can "perceive" targets that may be invisible because
hidden in fog by bouncing radar from them, as is discussed in the
next chapter on the detection of the speed of vehicles by radar.

If a sound wave strikes another medium, the energy from the sound wave causes this new medium to vibrate. An example of this might be the passing of a heavy truck in front of a house, which causes the windows to vibrate. This is the same principle upon which the human ear functions. The sound waves in the air cause the eardrum to vibrate. The vibrating motion of the eardrum is then converted into nerve impulses which are sent to the brain, where the impulses are perceived as sounds. Just as the brain can record sound, as sound, in our memory, so can we devise instruments that record sound waves as visual patterns. By looking at the "output" of these machines, we can "see" sound, or at least observe a pictorial representation of sound. The sound spectrograph is such an instrument.

The sound spectrograph made its appearance in 1942 as a result of research in the Bell Telephone Laboratories. It was devised as a tool for basic studies of speech signals as they related to communications services. Much of the original research concerned applications of the instrumentation and techniques to the war effort, but since the end of World War II the instrument has come to be widely used in many laboratories for research studies of sound, music and speech.

It records, in graphic form, the different frequencies and intensities which make up sound. For two sounds to be identical, they must be composed of the same sound wave frequencies at the same intensities. Variance in intensity, however, does not affect the frequency (or pitch) of sound. While working for the Bell System, Lawrence Kersta adapted the sound spectrograph to the process of identifying individuals by their speech, creating what he called the voiceprint identification method. A pictorial representation of a simple sentence is shown in Figure 57. Kersta proceeded from the premise that each person's voice is as unique as his fingerprints when subjected to spectrographic analysis.

THE THEORY OF VOICE UNIQUENESS

The claimed uniqueness of speech results from the process by which human speech is produced physiologically and from the process whereby one learns to speak. Kersta contends that voice individuality is founded in the mechanism of speech. The parts of the vocal tract which determine voice uniqueness are the vocal cavities

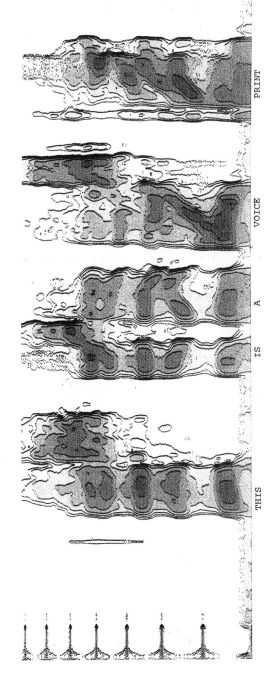

Figure 57. Courtesy: Voiceprint Laboratories

and the articulators. The vocal cavities are resonators which, much like organ pipes, cause energy to be reinforced in specific sound spectrum areas dependent upon their sizes. The major cavities affecting speech are the throat, nasal and two oral cavities formed in the mouth by positioning the tongue. The contribution of the vocal cavities to voice uniqueness lies in their size and the manner in which they are coupled, with the likelihood of two people having all vocal cavities in the same size and coupled identically being remote.

A still greater factor in determining voice uniqueness, according to Kersta, is the way in which the articulators are manipulated during speech. The articulators include the lips, teeth, tongue, soft palate and jaw muscles, whose controlled dynamic interplay results in intelligible speech, something that is not a spontaneous process but a studied process of imitation and trial and error. Figure 58 is a schematic representation of the vocal mechanism.

Kersta contends that the chance that two individuals would have the same dynamic use patterns for their articulators would be remote, and his overall claim to voice pattern uniqueness when sub-

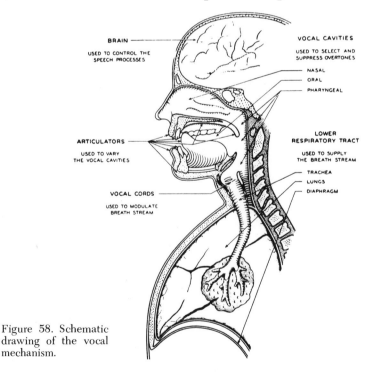

Figure 58. Schematic drawing of the vocal mechanism.

mitted to the sound spectrograph rests on the improbability that two speakers would have vocal cavity dimensions and articulator use patterns similar enough to confound voiceprint identification methods.

In applying his technique, Kersta uses two different kinds of voiceprints. They are bar voiceprints, showing the resonance bars of the voice with dimensions of time, frequency and loudness, and contour voiceprints, measuring levels of loudness, time and frequency in a shape much like a topographical map. The two different types of voiceprints are illustrated in Figure 59.

To arrive at a determination, it is required that a recording of questioned speech and a recording of known speech be available. Questioned speech might be a recording of a telephone bomb threat, of an incriminating admission or of an obscene telephone call made by an unknown person. A known speech sample is one recorded from a suspect.

To compare both for the purpose of determining whether the questioned speech was produced by the suspect, the spectrographic impressions of ten commonly used English cue words found in the questioned speech are visually compared with the spectrographic

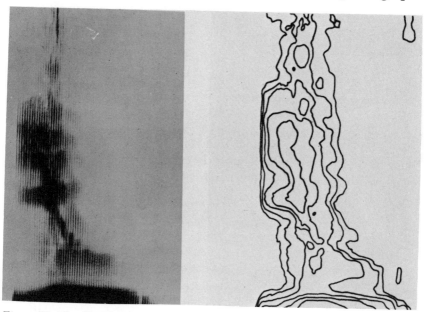

Figure 59. The illustration on the left is a bar voiceprint; the one on the right is a contour voiceprint. Courtesy: Voiceprint Laboratories

impressions of these same words in the known speech sample. The cue words used by Kersta are "the," "to," "and," "me," "on," "is," "you," "I," "it" and "a." If the spectrographic impressions of these words match in both samples, Kersta concludes that both speech samples were uttered by the same individual.

He claims that in his identification experiments in over 50,000 tests he obtained an accuracy greater than 99%. He also conducted a study to demonstrate that there are certain individual traits in the quality of voice of individuals even when speech production mechanisms may be expected to be identical and when environmental effects are similar, as in the case of identical twins, and that the individuality of these traits could be discovered even by the untrained. His "panel of experts" consisted of two seventeen-year-old high school girls who prior to the study had no knowledge of voiceprint techniques and whose scientific background consisted of high school science. Their only instruction in voiceprint techniques was that they were told to look for a pattern that looked most similar to another given pattern.

The "subjects" consisted of fifteen pairs of fraternal male twins and fifteen pairs of fraternal female twins. Fraternal twin voices were selected to enable the panelists to gain familiarity with the technique and note familial likenesses. A second group of subjects consisted of thirty identical twins. All twins, fraternal and identical, were under twelve years of age so that uniqueness of the voice before puberty would at the same time be demonstrated.

The high school panelists had an overall identification success score of 87%, according to Kersta, with an 84% score for females and a 90% score for males. Kersta then repeated the experiment using a female "expert" who at that time had eight months of experience in voiceprint identification but who had never studied the voices of identical twins. The technician's background included a B.A. in English with selected courses in linguistics. Kersta reports that this technician was able to identify sixty identical twins with only one error.

The Evaluation of Reliability

When Kersta first published a report on his voiceprint experiments in 1966, no one was in a position to challenge his claim of voice uniqueness. For some time thereafter, it was also difficult to test the accuracy of his findings, since he kept hidden some of the techniques he was using. Very soon after the "unveiling" of his system of voiceprint identification, a great number of other authorities (some of whom never had experience with the sound spectrograph) attacked both his claims of voice uniqueness and the obtainable accuracy results. It would appear that at present no authoritative scientific information is available, based on accepted acoustical principles applied to a broad enough population, to either support or deny Kersta's claims.

At the 80th meeting of the Acoustical Society of America in Houston, Texas, in November, 1970, Dr. Oscar Tosi of Michigan State University reported on his experiments with voice identification by the visual inspection of spectrograms. He concluded that the reliability of speaker identification varied according to the particular conditions included in the trial tests with a range of errors from .9% to 29.1%, using college students without extensive voiceprint identification experience as technicians.

Insofar as Kersta's standard test pattern for demonstrating the ease of identification (illustrated in Figure 60) was concerned, Tosi's findings did not produce a correspondingly high rate of accuracy. His tests were based on samples of speakers who did not attempt to disguise their voices, a factor which, according to Kersta, does not significantly affect spectrographic voice recognition. Dr. Tosi also concluded that the range of test errors had a tendency to discard the guilty rather than to accuse the innocent, but he suggested that further extensive testing would be necessary since the various persons participating in the voice identification tests could not consistently approach the degree of accuracy claimed by Kersta.

EVIDENTIAL PROBLEMS

A number of large metropolitan police departments have acquired voice spectrographs and have been training personnel in their use. The technique has been found to be extremely helpful as an investigative aid in identifying criminals who use the telephone to make obscene calls, to threaten to bomb public buildings and airlines, to make extortion threats, and to make ransom demands.

The first police application proved a suspect innocent: the voiceprints showed that he was not the depraved caller who had made violent death threats to a Connecticut family, even though the vic-

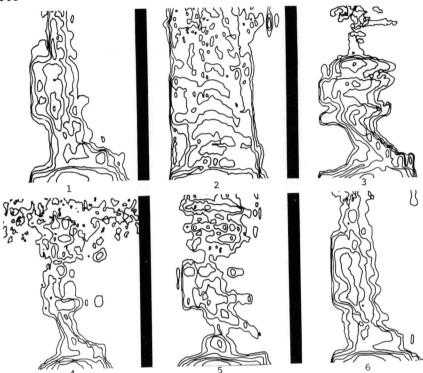

Figure 60. Contour voiceprints of five male speakers uttering the word "you." Voiceprints 1 and 6 were spoken by the same person. Courtesy: Voiceprint Laboratories

tims, upon hearing the suspect's voice, believed him to have been the caller. Subsequently, the true criminal was found and he pleaded guilty.

Kersta has testified about voiceprint evidence for the prosecution in a number of trials since 1966. The appellate courts, however, have not been satisfied that voiceprints should be admitted in evidence. The New Jersey reviewing court stated that there was no proof of general scientific acceptance of the voiceprint technique—a prerequisite to the admissibility of novel scientific test results. The California Court of Appeal has also refused to admit voiceprints as evidence. In an extensive opinion, reviewing the voluminous testimony of defense experts attacking Kersta's findings, the court decided that Kersta's claims about the accuracy of the voiceprint method are founded on theories and conclusions which have not yet been substantiated by accepted methods of scientific verification. (It must be pointed out that the defense experts, generally, had no experience with the sound spectrograph; they were professors of linguistics or speech and their testimony in effect was that the voiceprint technique was unknown rather than that it was unreliable.)

A breakthrough occurred on November 26, 1971, when a unanimous Minnesota Supreme Court decided that voiceprint techniques had become sufficiently reliable since the prior decisions to warrant admission into evidence of the test results. While this case, if followed by other courts, may reverse the trend to exclude the evidence set in prior decisions, it must be remembered that there is still considerable technical and scientific opposition to the claims for accuracy of the test's proponents. Since experimentation and research continues, this question may be resolved in the very near future. As an investigative tool, however, spectrographic voice recognition has already proved its great value as a process to eliminate suspects and furnish leads toward the discovery of other evidence of guilt.

Chapter 10

Speed Detection Devices

Almost everyone is familiar with the enormous toll in human lives and property damage that automobile accidents take every year. Because of the great number of motor vehicles which crowd the nation's roads, it is inevitable that accidents will occur. The causes are many; some are preventable, others are not. Among the causes are driver intoxication, fatigue, negligence and mechanical failure, to name but a few. Another significant one is excessive speed.

Once an accident has occurred and it becomes necessary to determine at what speed the driver was driving, there are a variety of means whereby the speed may be proved. One would be simply by eyewitness estimate; another might be by the testimony of a driver who was following or passed by the vehicle involved in the accident; and yet another might be a calculation of the speed of the vehicle involved in the accident by a study of the skid marks—a technique which affords considerable accuracy as to the speed a vehicle was going when the brakes were first applied.

In order to prevent accidents and to protect the motoring public and pedestrians alike, a number of means have been devised or adapted which are designed to catch speeders and prosecute them criminally for violations of the motor vehicle codes. Again, speed may be established by the trained observation of a traffic police officer, by police pursuit in a car so that the speed of the pursued vehicle can be established by reference to the police vehicle's speedometer, and by various mechanical devices, one of which consists of a rubber tube stretched across the highway which is connected to a box that measures speed on the basis of the interval elapsing between front wheel and rear wheel passage over the tube. The most effective means of speed detection, however, have been scientific ones, primarily radar speed detection and the fairly new VAS-CAR technique.

RADAR SPEED DETECTION

The radar speedmeter is probably the most common automatic speed detector currently used. Contemporary units were developed as an offshoot of military radar utilized during World War II to measure the height, speed and distance of various objects. The word "radar" is an acronym for RAdio Detection And Ranging, and is applied to both the technique and the equipment used. A radar unit is essentially composed of a transmitter and a receiver of radio waves.

The "pulse" type of radar, developed and used by the military, sends out a beam of radio microwaves in regular intervals which are reflected or bounced back to the receiver by the object detected. The waves move in both directions at the speed of light, which is a constant factor. Thus a computation of the time elapsed between the time of sending out the pulse wave and receiving it gives the distance of the objected detected.

The radar speedmeter operates in a distinct but similar manner to military radar. The components also include a transmitter-receiver, coupled to a specially designed voltmeter calibrated on a scale in mile-per-hour equivalents, and an optional graph recorder. The transmitter sends out a cone-shaped stream of radio wave crests continuously in the direction the speedmeter is pointed. The number of wave crests is constant, being the frequency of the radio wave. When the beam strikes an object, some of the beam is reflected back to the receiver part of the speedmeter. The reflection is called the "echo."

If the object is stationary, the frequency of the echo is identical to the frequency of the original transmitter beam. If the object is moving toward or away from the transmitter, the echo has a different frequency and the change in frequency varies directly with the speed of the moving object off which the echo is reflected. This change in frequency is part of an effect that Christian J. Doppler called attention to in 1842.

Everyone has observed the Doppler effect when driving past a car whose horn is blowing, or when standing still at a railroad crossing while a train passes by giving the crossing signal. The pitch or frequency appears to change in both situations, moving from a high pitch to a lower pitch just as one passes the car or as the train passes. So the Doppler effect is an apparent change in the frequency of a vibration which occurs when there is relative motion between the source of the vibration and the receiver of the vibration.

The Doppler effect is particularly suitable for measuring the speed of motor vehicles. When a car is moving along a road toward a radar speedmeter, it runs into some wave crests emitted by the speedmeter that it would not have run into until the next microsecond or so had it been standing still. To the car, the frequency of the transmitter seems to be higher than it actually is. In reflecting these waves toward the receiver of the radar speedmeter, the car becomes a moving source of waves of this slightly higher frequency. The receiver picks up the waves of the transmitter and the waves sent back by the car, thus forming a "beat" wave similar to the one produced by striking two piano keys simultaneously. By means of a simple formula calculated within the machine, the difference in the frequencies of the beat wave is determined to be directly proportional to the velocity of the car. The velocity is recorded in mile-per-hour equivalents on the meter face for the control officer's evaluation and record.

The technique of using radar speedmeters usually involves two police cars. First, one equipped with the apparatus, the "radar car," is parked alongside a road. The radar unit must be calibrated and checked for accuracy by one of several testing procedures. The second car is parked down the road from the radar car so that it will be in a position to apprehend speed limit violators. When a speeding car passes the radar car, the controlling officer communicates by radio with the "catch" car and describes the offender, giving the license number, if possible, and the speed registered. The first car records the speed and other data while the catch car stops the motorist and issues a summons for the violation.

Proper Operating Principles

The principles of the radar speedmeter are scientifically sound, yet the practical operation of these devices creates some problems.

Failure to permit the unit a minimum of ten minutes to warm up or having the needle of the meter register above zero before use gives inflated readings. X-ray or diathermy equipment in the vicinity can cause false readings. Movements of birds, trees and metal signs can affect readings. Usually, these effects are minimal unless their frequency corresponds to that of the moving target. Yet it is impossible to filter out the effect without also removing the target signal. The age of the unit can cause incorrect readings, though these would usually be lower than the actual speed of the vehicle tested. The angle of the radar car and the distance from the highway are also relevant factors which affect the accuracy of the speedmeter.

Radar operators have difficulty singling out the speeding vehicle in heavy traffic. Radar functions best in a relatively featureless background with isolated targets. The difficulty is greatest when utilizing radar on a multilane freeway during rush hour amid the extensive background of buildings and signs. For these and other obvious reasons, few police departments utilize radar speedmeters during rush hours in or near metropolitan areas. A radar speedmeter always registers the vehicle with the highest speed, so a reading corroborated by the testimony of a police officer is needed to identify the offending car and its speed.

The radar speedmeter is also subject to error if it is not operated properly, which includes sufficient testing to ensure accuracy. This is very important because many courts hold that untested radar equipment readings standing alone are insufficient to convict for speeding. What the proper testing requirements are varies with the equipment used, and also the requirements various states impose. Most states have rather strict requirements for testing; some require approval of the unit by state officials and periodic testing, as often as once every thirty days. The three basic methods of testing a radar unit for accuracy are internal tests, tuning fork tests and road tests using a vehicle with a calibrated speedometer.

The internal tests must be performed by an electronics technician and involve checking the oscillation input of the device. As has been alluded to, an extremely small variation in this input can produce a significant error in the speed reading. Based on the proposition that an oscillation variation of .1% produces a speed error of two miles per hour, it can readily be seen that an error in oscillation of a mere one percent produces a speed error of 20 miles per hour, an error that would most assuredly render the device useless as a means of enforcing speed laws.

Field-testing the radar speedmeter is a necessary verification of accurate operation. Two tests are used for this purpose. One is to run a vehicle with a calibrated speedometer past the radar unit and compare the speedometer reading in the "drive through" vehicle with the reading obtained on the radar meter. The second most commonly used test of accuracy requires the use of a tuning fork. Since the unit measures the Doppler effect, which is in turn a measurement of reflected frequency of vibration, any given frequency corresponds to a given speed as it would be recorded in the speedmeter. Tuning forks are available that are calibrated in almost all speeds from 15 mph to 100 mph in multiples of 5 mph. By holding several different tuning forks in front of the speedmeter and observing whether the recorded speed corresponds with that for which each tuning fork was designed, the field accuracy of the radar unit may be established. A number of states make such a testing procedure mandatory before and after use.

THE ADMISSIBILITY OF RADAR EVIDENCE

When radar evidence was first introduced, the courts required that technical testimony be offered to establish the scientific principle that radar is an accurate speed-measuring device. Only then would police officers be permitted to testify about radar speed readings. One of the early expert witnesses to appear in court was Dr. John M. Kopper, an electrical engineering teacher and research scientist at Johns Hopkins University. He had authored a number of articles relating to the soundness of the principles and reliability of the speedmeter radar apparatus. His views and writings had an important influence on the early acceptance by the courts of radar as a reliable instrument. As a result, the courts soon accepted radar as a reliable means of detecting the speed of a vehicle, and are no longer requiring scientific testimony about radar principles and reliability. But the courts have continued to require demonstrations of the proper operation and testing of each radar instrument and of the operator's qualifications to use it.

It must also be observed that some states have passed legislation requiring the posting of warning signs to indicate that radar is used to monitor speed. In those states, a courtroom demonstration must also be made that the proper signs existed on the highway leading to the place where the radar unit was stationed.

VASCAR SPEED DETECTION

VASCAR is an acronym for Visual Average Speed Computer And Record. It originated as a relatively simple device patented in 1958 in West Virginia by Arthur N. Marshall. The original device was purely mechanical and allowed for the measurement by a pursuit vehicle of the distance traveled by a suspect vehicle by simply having the pursuit vehicle travel the same distance while the device measured that distance. At the same time, a stopwatch measured the time it took the suspect vehicle to travel the known distance. The device offered a crude improvement on the conventional speedometer-odometer combination but left much to be desired. The officer still had to compute the speed of the suspect vehicle using time-distance information obtained from the device and the stopwatch, and he was forced to observe two instruments while attempting to watch the suspect vehicle at the same time.

When the Federal Sign and Signal Corporation assumed the manufacturing and marketing responsibility in 1967, VASCAR quickly developed into a sophisticated and highly refined electronic digital computer. Acceptance and use of the device has grown tremendously since that time. VASCAR is presently in use in 30 states and Puerto Rico.

VASCAR operates on the simple and scientifically proven formula that average velocity equals the distance traveled divided by the time taken to travel that distance, or, as expressed in a formula, $AV = \frac{D}{T}$. So it should encounter no difficulty meeting court standards. Three modules make up the VASCAR device: the odometer module, the control module with its readout portion and the computer module (see Figure 61.)

The odometer module measures distance and is inserted in the odometer cable at the transmission. It is the only part of the instrument that needs a mechanical connection to the police vehicle that is using the equipment. It consists of a photosensitive diode, an exciter lamp and a light-interrupter disk driven by the speedometer cable.

The control module is used by the operator to activate the distance and time measuring device. It has two single-pole, double-throw switches for controlling time and distance inputs, a black momentary contact switch for resetting to zero, a red momentary

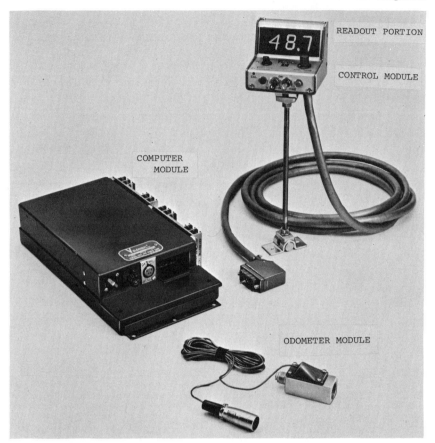

Figure 61. The components of the VASCAR unit. Courtesy: Federal Sign and Signal Corporation

contact switch to control the distance-storage function, and a multi-turn screw potentiometer for calibration adjustments. The control module is mounted on a rigid stand between the driver's seat and the front passenger's seat of the police car (see Figure 62). The readout portion consists of three seven-line digital displays utilizing 25 MA tungsten filament lamps, a lamp to indicate speeds in excess of 99.9 mph and a continuously lighted decimal point.

The computer module, which is generally located under the front seat on the driver's side, consists of electrical circuitry to store time and distance information, to provide an accurate time base, to compute average velocity and to provide switching for the digital display of the readout portion of the control module.

Figure 62. The unit that contains the control module and the visual readout portion is within easy reach of the police officer. Courtesy: Federal Sign and Signal Corporation.

The operator of the device can measure distance by turning on the distance switch when the police car reaches a predetermined point on the highway; he turns off the same switch when he reaches another predetermined point farther down the road. The time element can be stored in the computer by turning on another electrical switch when the target vehicle reaches the first of the same points, and the switch is turned off when it reaches the second point. The only component of the unit which the operator is concerned with during field use is the control module. A switch on the left of the operator is for measuring distance, which is always measured by the police car; a switch on the right is for time, and is always measured on the target vehicle.

In operation, this is what the officer does. When the violator's vehicle reaches a certain location or reference point on the road, such as a painted line across the pavement, the time switch is turned on, thus activating the time circuitry in the computer. When the police car equipped with VASCAR reaches the same point, the operator turns on the distance switch, activating the distance circuitry to record the distance being measured by the police car through the odometer module connected to the speedometer cable. As the target vehicle reaches a second point, such as another line across the road, the time switch is turned off. The time that it has taken the target vehicle to travel between the two points has been measured and put into the computer.

As soon as the police vehicle reaches the same second point, the distance switch is turned off, and the distance between the same two points has then been measured and put into the computer. The speed of the violator's vehicle is electronically computed and instantly displayed on the control module readout in miles per hour. It is not necessary for the officer to take his eyes off the road at any time during the clocking procedure except to glance at the resulting readout speed. This speed will remain on the readout portion until the officer clears the computer by pushing the reset button. This method of clocking results in an average speed calculation; the average speed is never higher than the peak speed the vehicle reached.

The reference points an officer can use as location markers are many and varied: shadows being cast by stationary objects along the highway, guard rails, beginnings of crossovers and intersections, rural roadside mailboxes and so forth. The unit can be used in sunlight, on overcast days and even at night when driving requires the use of headlights.

The accuracy of the combined modules is tested by the manufacturer to a maximum variation of one-tenth of one percent before they are shipped. This test is based on an average velocity of 100 mph. Installation is purely mechanical with the odometer module being attached to the speedometer cable. There is no need to tamper with the mechanical operation of any of the modular units. If one of the units is damaged by being dropped the whole device will fail. There will be no possibility of an error; it simply will not work. The readout portion will read 00.1 and will continue to do so until repairs are made and the device is recalibrated. This same figure, 00.1, remains on the digital display until the unit has had sufficient time to warm up. The warm-up period is important since the most sensitive portion of the device, the oscillator, must be maintained at a constant temperature in its case. If the temperature varies, the figure 00.1 will appear on the digital display, indicating an error. If the operator tries to feed in either time or distance twice during the same computation, the device will again read 00.1, indicating the error. The maximum capacity of the computer is 6.5 minutes and 5.5 miles.

All VASCAR operators must be certified before they are allowed to use the device. The certification process involves classroom training of about one day, training on the road and the equivalent of one-half day of instruction in nighttime operation of the device. The student operator then spends approximately thirty days using the device, during which time he may issue warnings to motorists who, on the basis of his operation of the device, appear to be speeding. At the conclusion of his training period the operator is tested by his instructor, using a different vehicle, and must undergo a new series of examinations.

THE ADMISSIBILITY OF VASCAR EVIDENCE

The only possible failing of the VASCAR device rests in the operator, which is true of most sources of scientific evidence. If the operator is carefully trained and uses a properly tested unit, though, his testimony as to the speed of a violator's vehicle, determined on the basis of VASCAR data, should be readily admissible in court.

Because of the relative novelty of the technique, no significant court pronouncements on the highest state and federal judicial levels have been made so far. But VASCAR evidence has been accepted in a number of trials, usually after the foundation for admissibility was laid by experts from the manufacturer who explained to the court and jury the workings of the VASCAR device and testified to its scientific reliability.

Chapter 11

The Polygraph ("Lie Detector") Technique*

To the average police officer, the polygraph, better known as the "lie detector," is all too often thought of as a mechanical device that will produce a clear signal of deception whenever a question is answered untruthfully. Or he may have an entirely different viewpoint and discount altogether the notion that deception can be detected with the use of any kind of instrumentation. Both positions are unsupportable.

Although no mechanical device exists that will in and of itself detect lies, it is a demonstrable fact that there are instruments that are capable of recording various physiological changes which may serve as the basis for a reliable diagnosis of truth or deception. They are technically known as polygraphs, and the procedure by which they are utilized for diagnostic purposes is known as the polygraph technique.

THE INSTRUMENT

The two principal features of a polygraph are (a) a pneumatically operated recorder of changes in respiration and (b) a similar recorder of changes in blood pressure and pulse. The recordings of these two physiological changes are the most valuable of any that are presently obtainable.

There is also a unit for recording what is known as the galvanic skin reflex. It is presumably the result of changes in the activity of the sweat pores in a person's hands. An additional unit is available

° The illustrations in this chapter are from Reid and Inbau, *Truth and Deception: The Polygraph* ("*Lie-Detector*") *Technique,* Williams & Wilkins (Baltimore), 1966. Mr. Reid and his colleagues also cooperated in the preparation of the chapter.

for recording muscular movements and pressures. Any instrument that consists of only one of these units is inadequate for actual case testing.

The body attachments by which the respiration and the blood pressure and pulse recordings are obtained are as follows:

1. A "pneumograph tube," which with the aid of a beaded chain is fastened around the chest or abdomen of the person being tested
2. A blood pressure cuff, of the type used by physicians, which is fastened around the subject's upper arm
3. Electrodes, fastened to the hand or fingers, through which an imperceptible amount of electrical current is passed for the purpose of obtaining the galvanic skin reflex.

No body attachments are required for recording body movements and pressures. They are obtained by means of metal bellows located under the arms and the seat of the chair occupied by the subject.

All of the foregoing units, as well as the entire polygraph itself, are shown in Figure 63, which also illustrates the relative positions of the subject and the examiner during an examination.

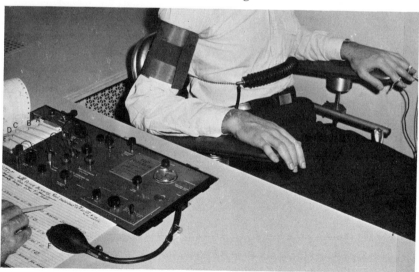

Figure 63. Instrument panel and attachments of the Reid polygraph.
A. Pen for recording arm movements and muscular pressure.
B. Respiration recording pen.
C. Galvanic skin reflex recording pen.
D. Blood pressure-pulse recording pen.
E. Pen for recording thigh movements and muscular pressures.
F. Bulb for inflating blood pressure cuff.

The Examiner

Because the polygraph technique involves a diagnostic procedure rather than a mere mechanical operation, a prime requisite to its effectiveness and reliability is examiner competence. An examiner must be a person of intelligence, with a good educational background—preferably a college degree. And since he will be dealing with persons in delicate situations, he must also possess suitable personality characteristics, which might be categorized as the ability "to get along" well with others and to be persuasive in his dealings with them.

The training must have been received on an internship basis under the guidance of a competent, experienced examiner who has a sufficient volume of actual cases to permit the trainee to make frequent observations of polygraph examinations and to conduct his own examinations under the instructor's personal supervision. Along with this the trainee should have read, and received instruction in, the pertinent phases of psychology and physiology. Attention must also have been given to the detailed study and analysis of a considerable number of polygraph test records in actual cases in which the true facts of truthfulness or deception were later established by independent evidence. The time required for this individualized training is approximately six months. There are, unfortunately, relatively few persons holding themselves out as polygraph examiners who have the required qualifications, and particularly with respect to the internship training that is so essential to an adequate utilization of the technique.

The Examination Room

Polygraph examinations must be conducted in a quiet, private room. Extraneous noises, or the presence of investigators or other spectators in the room, would produce distractions that could seriously affect the examination and the diagnosis.

The Pretest Interview

Before administering a polygraph examination, a competent examiner will explain to the subject the purpose and nature of the examination and something about the instrument itself. Also during the pretest interview, the examiner will seek to condition the subject for the test by relieving the apprehensions of the truthful subject as well as satisfying the lying subject of the effectiveness of the technique. Another reason for the pretest interview is the opportunity it affords for the formulation of the test questions, particularly the ones which will serve as "controls."

During the pretest interview the examiner must remain completely objective with regard to the subject's truthfulness or deception. Under no circumstance should he indulge in an interrogation at that time. To do so then would seriously impair the validity of the technique, because of the incompatibility of any accusation or insinuation of lying and a subsequent scientific test avowedly designed to determine the very fact of truthfulness or deception. Interrogation is appropriate only *after* the results of the polygraph examination have indicated deception.

THE TEST QUESTIONS

Control Questions

Indispensable to a proper polygraph examination is the development and use of control questions. A control question is unrelated to the matter under investigation but is of a similar, though less serious, nature. In all probability, the subject will lie in answering it both before and during the test, or at least his answer will give him some concern with respect to either its truthfulness or its accuracy. For instance, in a burglary case the control question might be: "Have you ever stolen anything?" or, "Since you were 21 years old, have you ever stolen anything?" or, "Except for what you've told me, have you ever stolen anything?" The recorded physiological response or lack of response to the control question (in respiration, blood pressure-pulse, etc.) is then compared with what appears in the tracings when the subject was asked questions pertaining to the matter under investigation.

Relevant Questions

Questions relating to the particular matter under investigation are known as "relevant" questions.

Irrelevant Questions

In order to ascertain the subject's "norm" under the test conditions, he is asked several questions that have no bearing on the case investigation. These are known as "irrelevant" questions. An example of such a question is one regarding the place where the test is being conducted—for instance, "Are you in Chicago now?"

Test Procedure

Prior to the test the subject is told precisely what the questions will be, and he is also assured that no questions will be asked about any other offense or matter than that which has been discussed with him by the examiner. Surprise has no part in a properly conducted test.

The following is a list of the kinds and arrangement of questions which are asked during a typical polygraph test and to which the subject is to answer with a "yes" or a "no." They are based on a hypothetical robbery-murder case in which the victim is John Jones and the suspect is Joe "Red" Blake.

1. Do they call you "Red"? [The pretest interview has disclosed that he is generally called "Red."]
2. Are you over 21 years of age? [Or reference is made to some other age unquestionably but reasonably, and not ridiculously, below that of the subject.]
3. Did you steal John Jones' watch last Saturday night?
4. Are you in Chicago now?
5. Did you shoot John Jones last Saturday night?
6. Besides what you told about, did you ever steal anything else?
7. Did you ever go to school?
8. Were those your footprints near John Jones' body?
9. Do you know who shot John Jones?
10. Did you ever steal anything from a place where you worked?

The time interval between each question is fifteen or twenty seconds.

One such test does not constitute a polygraph examination. There must be at least three and usually more tests of a similar nature before a diagnosis can be attempted. The entire examination may take approximately one hour.

At the risk of oversimplification, it may be said that if the subject responds more to the control questions than to the relevant questions, he is considered to be telling the truth with regard to the matter under investigation. On the other hand, a greater response to the relevant questions is suggestive of deception.

The following are illustrations of a number of case records which reveal responses that are considered indicative (a) of truth telling and (b) of lying. They contain only respiration and blood pressure-pulse tracings; subsequent ones will illustrate the criteria that may appear in the tracings of galvanic skin reflex and of muscular movements and pressures.

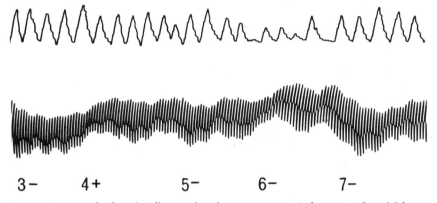

3 −   4 +   5 −   6 −   7 −

Figure 64. Record of truth-telling embezzlement suspect. Indications of truthfulness in both respiration and blood pressure-pulse.

Questions 3 and 5 pertained to the embezzlement of a large sum of money, 3 being "Do you know who stole the missing money?" and 5 being "Did you steal the missing money?" Questions 4 and 7 were irrelevant. Observe the suppression in respiration and the blood pressure rise at control question 6, when the subject was asked: "Did you ever steal anything?" His answer was a lie, according to the subject's later admission.

On the basis of the above control question test record, the examiner was able to report that the subject was telling the truth about the missing money. The conclusion was later confirmed.

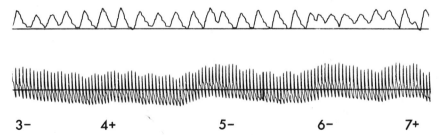

3 −   4 +   5 −   6 −   7 +

Figure 65. Record of truth-telling complainant in rape case. Indications of truthfulness in respiration alone.

Questions 4 and 7 were irrelevant. At 3 and 5 the subject was asked whether she had consented to the acts, as alleged by the two accused young men. Her "no" answers did not produce significant responses, whereas 6, the control question, did. At 6 she was asked whether she had ever had sexual intercourse with anyone prior to the date of the alleged rape. Her response in respiration at that point clearly indicated that her "no" answer was a lie. Based on the lack of any comparable response at 3 and 5, the examiner concluded that the accusation of rape was truthful.

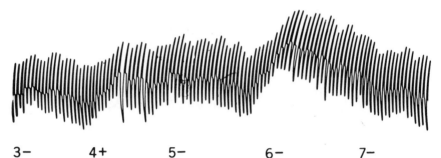

3−	4+	5−	6−	7−

Figure 66. Record of a truth-telling arson suspect. Indications of truthfulness in blood pressure-pulse alone.

Questions 3 and 5 pertained to an arson for which the motive was destruction of the employer's books and records in order to conceal an embezzlement; 4 and 7 were irrelevant; 6 was the control question: "Did you ever steal anything?" The only significant response appeared in the blood pressure tracing at control question 6, a known lie reaction, since shortly after the test the subject admitted having stolen money at various times and places. In view of the reaction to the known lie at 6 and the lack of any response at arson questions 3 and 5, the proper interpretation was one of truth telling regarding the arson.

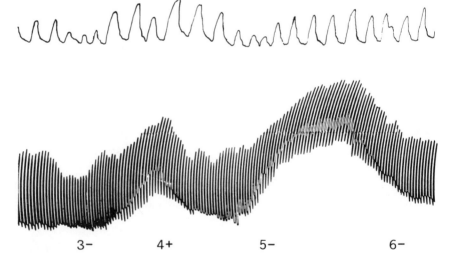

3−	4+	5−	6−

Figure 67. Record of a lying burglary suspect. Indications of lying in both respiration and blood pressure-pulse.

Questions 3 and 5 pertained to a burglary; 4 was irrelevant; 6 was the control question: "Did you ever steal anything?" The subject's answer of "no" was a known lie. Deceptive responses appear in both respiration and blood pressure at 3 and 5.

The lying regarding the burglary was of paramount concern to this subject, while his general stealing was of no consequence. This is the reverse of the situation of a person who is telling a truth regarding the main issue; his principal concern on the test is the control question lie.

162

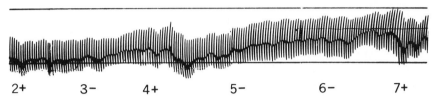

2+   3−   4+   5−   6−   7+

Figure 68. Record of lying male suspect in aggravated assault upon a woman. Indications of lying in respiration alone.

Questions 3 and 5 were relevant; 2, 4, and 7 were irrelevant; 6 was the control question: "Since November, did you think of dating any other woman than your wife?"

In the respiration tracing, observe the normal breathing at 2, the rise in the base line beginning at 3, the relief in respiration at 4, a further base line rise at 5, then the descent shortly after 6 and a return to the original level at 7. Specific, as well as general base line changes such as these are reliable indications of lying to the relevant questions, 3 and 5.

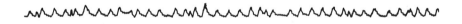

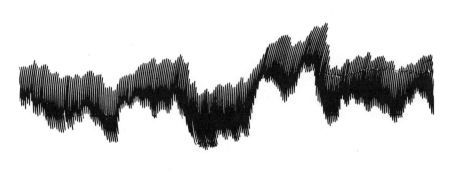

1+   2+   3−   4+   5−   6−   7+

Figure 69. Record of a lying embezzlement suspect. Indications of lying in blood pressure-pulse alone.

Questions 3 and 5 pertain to an embezzlement; 1, 2, 4, and 7 were irrelevant; 6 was the control question: "Besides what you told about, did you ever steal anything else?" The specific responses at 3 and 5, and the much lesser response to 6, were indicative of deception about the embezzlement.

163

Peak of Tension Tests

When a person who is to undergo a polygraph examination has not been informed of all the important details of the offense under investigation, the examiner can conduct as part of his examination what is known as a "peak of tension" test. It consists of the asking of a series of questions in which only one refers to some detail of the offense, such as the amount of money stolen or the kind of object taken or the implement used to commit the offense—something that would be unknown to the subject unless he himself committed the crime or unless he had been told about it by someone else. For instance, if a suspected thief has not been told about the exact amount of money involved, he may be asked a series of questions which refer to various amounts, one of which will be the actual amount stolen. The theory behind the peak of tension test is that if the person tested is the one who took the money, for instance, he will be apprehensive about the question referring to that amount, whereas an innocent person would not have such a particularized concern.

Before conducting a peak of tension test, the examiner prepares a list of about seven questions, among which, near the middle, is the question pertaining to the actual detail. The list is then read off to the subject, and he is informed that during the test questions will be asked in that precise order. A truth-telling subject, unaware of the accuracy of any one question, will not ordinarily be concerned about one more than any of the others. On the other hand, a lying subject will have that question in mind as the test is being conducted and, in anticipation of it, he is apt to experience a buildup of tension that will climax at the crucial question—in other words, that will reach a "peak of tension."

The appearance in a polygraph record of this peak of tension in the blood pressure tracing is illustrated in Figure 70. Figure 71 indicates the value of galvanic skin reflex tracing in peak of tension testing. (This additional tracing is also helpful in the regular control question test procedure, in which the subject is instructed to answer test questions silently to himself rather than audibly to the examiner, but the intricacies of this aspect of polygraph examining are beyond the scope of the present publication.)

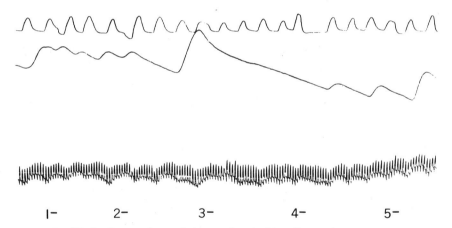

$10 – $20 – $30 – $40 – $50 – $60 – $70 –

Figure 70. The "Peak of tension" test record of a purse snatcher.

In this case, a woman had been assaulted and robbed of her purse, containing $47. The suspect was not told of the amount of money the purse contained. On this peak of tension test he was asked whether the purse contained $10, $20 and so forth, as shown on the above record. To all the questions he was instructed to say, "no." Observe the peak of tension on his blood pressure just before the $50. (It might even be suggested that the peak is at the exact amount of $47.)

After the examiner showed the record to the subject, with the numbers concealed, and asked him to point out the highest point (that is, the "peak of tension") in the blood pressure tracing, he did, and when the numbers were exposed he exclaimed: "Holy smoke, right at $47! *What* a machine!" He then promptly admitted having committed the robbery and the theft of that amount of money.

1 –   2 –   3 –   4 –   5 –

Figure 71. "Peak of tension" revealed in a galvanic skin reflex tracing.

The subject was a maid in a physician's home from which a blue envelope containing a considerable sum of money disappeared. On the above test, the subject, who professed not to have seen the envelope and not to know the color, was asked the following questions: (1) Was the missing envelope brown? (2) Was the missing envelope red? (3) Was the missing envelope blue? (4) Was the missing envelope yellow? (5) Was the missing envelope gray?

Observe the pronounced peak of tension in the G.S.R. tracing (the middle one) at 3, which referred to the blue envelope. Confronted with an actual display of this record, the subject admitted that she stole the money and returned it in the same blue envelope.

165

Lying Revealed by Efforts to Distort Polygraph Tracings

In addition to the normal indications of truth or deception in the various polygraph tracings, lying may be revealed by a subject's efforts to distort recordings or, in other words, "to beat the machine." For illustrations of such attempts, see Figures 72 and 73. The polygraph unit can also record more subtle and perhaps unintentional movements and pressures. Figure 74 shows the revealing nature of the tracing of muscular activities.

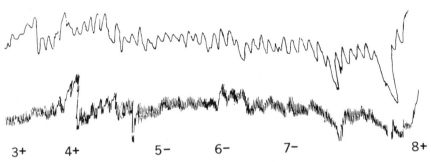

3+   4+   5−   6−   7−   8+

Figure 72. Record of a murderer's deliberately distorted tracings.
   During the examination of this subject, who was being questioned concerning the death of his wife, the examiner observed a flexing of the biceps muscle and some abnormally heavy breathing at various times throughout his first test. A repetition of the test was accompanied by the same behavior on the part of the subject. The records contained erratic respiratory and blood pressure tracings, and there was little doubt that they represented a deliberate effort to evade detection. Subsequently, the subject admitted that he had attempted to distort his record in order to confuse the examiner.

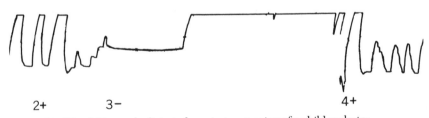

2+   3−   4+

Figure 73. The deliberately distorted respiratory tracing of a child molester.
   The subject was a university graduate student who had been accused of taking indecent liberties with a child. At relevant question 3 he held his breath for a full 60 seconds!
   Although respiratory blocks of from 5 to 15 seconds may represent true, natural deceptive responses, the duration of this respiratory block was clearly indicative of deliberate distortion, which the subject later admitted to be the case.

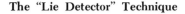
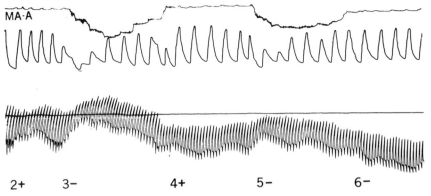

Figure 74. A record indicating the value of tracings of muscular movements and pressures in instances of attempts "to beat the machine."
  The record of a subject suspected of defacing a cemetery gravestone. Although the specific respiratory responses at relevant questions 3 and 5 are in themselves strongly indicative of deception, that diagnosis is rendered all the more certain by reason of the evidence of arm muscular activity at MA-A, when the subject was asked the same relevant questions 3 and 5.

THE EFFECT OF NERVOUSNESS ON EXAMINATION RESULTS

One of the most frequently asked questions about the polygraph technique is the effect of extreme nervousness. First of all, the pretest interview lessens the apprehension of a truthful, tense or nervous subject. Secondly, a subject whose nervousness persists will reveal that factor by the uniformly irregular nature of his polygraph tracings; in other words, physiological changes or disturbances induced only by nervousness usually appear on the polygraph record without relationship to any particular question or questions. They are usually of no greater magnitude—or, in any event, not consistently so—when relevant questions are asked than when irrelevant or control questions are asked. Finally, and most importantly, the employment of control questions offers great security against a misrepresentation of reactions caused by nervousness.

EXAMINATION RESULTS AND ACCURACY

In the examination of approximately twenty-five percent of the subjects presented to a competent polygraph examiner, truthfulness or deception may be so clearly disclosed by the nature of the reactions to relevant or control questions that the examiner will be able to point them out to any layman and satisfy him of their significance. In approximately sixty-five percent of the cases, however, the indications are not that clear; they are sufficiently subtle in appearance and in significance to require expert interpretation. In about ten percent of the cases, the examiner may be unable to make any diagnosis at all because of a subject's physiological or psychological characteristics or because of other inhibiting factors.

The accuracy of the polygraph technique is difficult to estimate. In many cases, the truth about who committed an offense may never be learned from confessions or from subsequently developed factual evidence. Proof is often lacking, therefore, that the examiner in any given case is either right or wrong in his diagnosis. One of the present authors (Inbau) and John E. Reid, his co-author of *Truth and Deception: The Polygraph ("Lie-Detector") Technique* (1966), are confident, on the basis of the testing of over 40,000 subjects by John E. Reid and Associates, that the polygraph technique, when properly applied by a trained competent examiner, is very accurate in its indications. The relatively few errors that do occur favor the innocent, since the known mistakes in diagnosis almost always involve a failure to detect deception rather than a diagnosis of lying on the part of a truth-telling subject.

THE LEGAL STATUS OF POLYGRAPH EXAMINATION RESULTS

The general rule at the present time is that the results of a polygraph examination are not usable as evidence in either a criminal or a civil case. The only current exception occurs in cases in which the prosecuting attorney and the defendant and his attorney (or the litigants and their attorneys in a civil case) agree in advance of the examination to permit the results to be admitted as evidence. Admissions or confessions made before, during or after a polygraph examination are admissible, provided that submission to the test was voluntary and that other legal requirements for interrogation (for instance, the Miranda warnings) have been met.

In their book, Reid and Inbau advocate the use of test results, even without a prior agreement to that effect, provided that (1) the examiner possesses a college degree; (2) the examiner has received at least six months of internship training under an experienced, competent examiner or examiners with a sufficient volume of case work to afford frequent supervised testing in actual case situations;

(3) the witness has at least five years of experience as a specialist in the field of polygraph examinations; and (4) the examiner's testimony is based on polygraph records that he produces in court and which are available for cross-examination. In any jury trial in which the test results are admitted as evidence, the court should instruct the jury that they should not consider the polygraph examiner's opinion as conclusive, but that they are privileged to consider his opinion along with all of the other evidence in the case and to give the opinion whatever weight and effect they think it reasonably deserves.

In concluding this discussion of the legal status of the results of polygraph examinations, mention should be made of the law with respect to a police officer being required to submit to a polygraph examination as part of an internal departmental investigation. Unless there is some legislative bar, a police officer's refusal to submit to such an examination pertaining to a matter directly related to his police activities justifies his dismissal.

THE POLICE INVESTIGATOR'S COOPERATION

Full effectiveness of the polygraph technique as an investigative aid can be achieved only through its proper utilization. To accomplish this objective there are several things that an investigator should and should not do whenever he contemplates the assistance of a polygraph examiner in the course of a case investigation.

First of all—and this applies to ordinary interrogations as well as to polygraph examinations—whenever a person under investigation offers an alibi it should be checked out immediately, and certainly before he undergoes a polygraph examination. If the alibi is found to be valid there is no need to administer a polygraph examination to him, unless for the purpose of ascertaining whether or not he is concealing information about the actual perpetrator of the crime. If the alibi check establishes its invalidity the subject may be confronted with that fact; if he offers no satisfactory explanation for it arrangements should be made for a polygraph examination to determine if he is involved in the crime and the extent of his involvement. (Investigators should be mindful, of course, of the possibility, even though unlikely, that a person may give a false alibi for some reason other than to conceal guilt—as, for instance, when a married man who is suspected of murdering a woman gives a false alibi to conceal the fact that at the time of the murder he was in the company of some other woman.)

Although the above suggestion for alibi checking may seem too elementary to mention, we have offered it anyway because of the frequency with which polygraph examiners encounter cases in which, either just before or after an examination, the subject offers an alibi that only then is to be checked out. Much time and expense could be spared by adhering to a standard practice of investigating an alibi before seeking a polygraph examination to determine whether or not the suspect is telling the truth when he denies having committed the offense in question.

So that a polygraph examiner may use the previously described peak of tension test as part of his examination, the police investigator should not reveal to the suspect the details of the crime. In other words, he should not (and there is usually no need to) disclose to the suspect the kind of implement used in a killing or the particular window through which a place was entered or the amount of money or the kind of object taken in the course of a robbery or burglary. By withholding such information whenever he can, the investigator assists the polygraph examiner, and the ultimate result of the examination will be more dependable. Moreover, the withholding by police investigators of certain details about a crime may be of considerable value and comfort as a check on the validity of a subsequently obtained confession. For instance, if a murder suspect has not been told what kind of implement was used in the killing or where it was thrown or hidden after the crime, a revelation of such a detail by the confessor is excellent evidence of the truthfulness of his confession.

When the services of a competent polygraph examiner are available and contemplated, the investigator should submit the suspect for an examination *early* in the course of the investigation rather than as a last resort. This may result in the quick elimination of innocent suspects and a concentration of effort with regard to the guilty one. In any event, the usefulness of a polygraph examination is greatly diminished if it is conducted after an extensive interrogation in which the subject has been dealt with as though guilty. A protracted and intensive interrogation may render a suspect psychologically unfit for a polygraph examination, at least for some time thereafter.

Following a brief, unpressured interview with a suspect whose guilt is not clearly indicated by the circumstances of the case or by what he has admitted, the investigator should *suggest* a lie detector test "to clear this whole matter up one way or another." Upon an expressed willingness to do so, the necessary arrangements should be made for the examination. If the suspect refuses, his refusal may reasonably be considered an indication of guilt, or at least suggestive of the possibility that he is concealing pertinent information about the offense. This, of course, is not a hard and fast rule, but it does warrant a temporary belief that the suspect should be thoroughly investigated.

A person who is to be given a polygraph examination should be in as near a normal physical and mental state as possible. The following requirements must be satisfied:

1. The subject must be reasonably well rested; otherwise, his fatigue may render him mentally dull, not alert enough to fully appreciate the importance and significance of the test questions.

2. The subject must not be in a state of hunger or thirst; otherwise, his attention will be focused upon that condition more than upon the examination procedure. Furthermore, if a confession subsequently results, it may well be declared invalid on the basis of involuntariness.

3. Before his examination a subject should be permitted, or even invited, to use toilet facilities; otherwise, his predominant concern may be his elimination needs rather than his deception, if he is guilty. Here again, physical discomfort could adversely affect a subsequent confession's admissibility.

4. Finally, as already suggested, a lengthy or intensive interrogation prior to a polygraph examination should be avoided.

As for all persons in custody, or those who have been "deprived of their freedom in any significant way," the Miranda warnings must precede any interrogation or polygraph examination. In other situations, however, the warnings are not required prior to an interrogation or examination. But if at any time a decision is made to place a person in custody, or if the circumstances reasonably indicate to him that he is no longer at liberty to leave, the Miranda warnings are required.

Appendix

An Outline of the Rules for Handling Physical Evidence

Reprinted with permission of J. Edgar Hoover, Director, Federal Bureau of Investigation, from *FBI Law Enforcement Bulletin*, July, 1954.

This article is a discussion of the mechanics of identification, preservation, submission, laboratory examination, and court presentation of physical evidence in criminal matters. Physical evidence may be defined as any article or material found during an investigation which may assist in the solution of the case and the prosecution of the guilty.

Purpose

Our purpose here is to outline in general the various procedures which experience has proved to be sound with respect to the successive steps involved in handling physical evidence from the time of its collection to court presentation. Most law enforcement officers will be familiar with some of the points to be covered but others may never have come to their attention.

Identification

Much of the material collected during the investigation may prove to be of little value as the case approaches the trial stage. Nevertheless, the same care and attention must prevail with respect to each and every item no matter how large or small or seemingly unimportant it may appear at the time. It is essential that every piece of material collected be properly identified and placed in an adequate container by the person who recovers it. These containers may take the form of pill boxes, powder boxes, test tubes, cellophane envelopes or any other form of closure.

There is no one method by which all items can be marked for future identification. Where possible, personal identification marks should be placed on each item prior to sealing it in its container. When not practical to mark the evidence itself, the container should be appropriately identified. For detailed instructions on how to identify, preserve, wrap and transmit physical evidence to the FBI Laboratory the investigator may refer to "Suggestions for Handling of Physical Evidence," a copy of which will be forwarded upon request made to the Director, Federal Bureau of Investigation, United States Department of Justice, Washington 25, D.C. [The chart contained therein is printed at the end of this article. Editor]

Preservation

Since physical evidence may consist of such a variety of material, it can be readily understood that a complete and detailed discussion is not possible here. This matter is specifically discussed in the publication just mentioned and remarks are contained therein with respect to nearly all items of physical evidence which might be encountered during an investigation.

The problem of preservation, however, is basic in the investigative field and one can ill afford to overlook its importance to the overall structure of the case under investigation.

FBI Laboratory Examinations

In many cases physical evidence collected during the investigation of the case will require laboratory examination. The facilities of the FBI Laboratory are made available without charge to all duly constituted Federal, State, county, and municipal agencies of the United States and its Territorial possessions in connection with their official investigations of criminal matters.

In offering these facilities, the limitations on their use have been kept to a minimum in an effort to be of as much assistance as possible in the proper administration of justice; however, experience has demonstrated the desirability of the policy that these facilities not be used to duplicate the work which has been or is to be done by others. This policy is desirable not only to eliminate duplication of effort but also to insure the examination of evidence in the condition at the time of recovery, enabling the proper interpretation to be placed on the examiner's findings and the subsequent court presentation and testimony.

Evidence for examination must be submitted by a duly constituted Federal, State, county or municipal agency in connection with the official investigation of a criminal matter. The evidence to be examined, as well as any other evidence in the same case, shall not have been previously subjected to the same type of technical examination and will not be so subjected on behalf of such agency or related agency. If it is known that there has been or is to be an examination on behalf of the defendant, details should be set forth where known. Since in making examinations it is necessary to know that these policies are being followed, certain pertinent information should be included in the letter of transmittal.

Letter of Transmittal

Unnecessary correspondence may be avoided in connection with a request for Laboratory study of the physical evidence and the examination will be expedited if the following information is incorporated in each letter of request:

(1) Letters should be prepared on the letterhead of the organization requesting the examination.

(2) The letter should be addressed to the Director, Federal Bureau of Investigation, Washington 25, D.C., Attention: FBI Laboratory.

(3) The letter should be prepared in duplicate, one copy to be included in each package of evidence forwarded.

(4) Set out the full name or names of the subject and the victim, including the offense and the date and place where it occurred.

(5) Set forth a brief statement concerning the circumstances of the case.

(6) Individually list the various items of evidence being forwarded and how shipment is being made.

(7) Set forth what should be sought in examination with respect to each specimen submitted.

(8) State whether any evidence in this case has been subjected to the same type of technical examination as that requested.

(9) Set forth any special instructions concerning return of the evidence, extra copies of the report or any other special consideration not covered elsewhere.

Transmittal of Evidence

As can be appreciated, it is not possible in this limited space to describe in detail the methods employed in the packing of all types and kinds of evidence which will be encountered during case investigations. In general it can be stated that each item of evidence should be separately wrapped and identified in such a way that the person responsible for the identification can properly make identification whenever required to do so.

Evidence is ordinarily received in the laboratory in one of the following manners:

(1) *Included with or attached to the letter of transmittal.*—When this method is utilized the material being submitted is not large or bulky and can be included conveniently with the letter of transmittal. In each case the specimens should be securely sealed in an envelope and marked as an enclosure in order that the contents are not disturbed in opening the envelope to obtain the letter of transmittal.

(2) *Evidence may be shipped separately and apart from the letter of transmittal.*—When this method is followed, a copy of the letter of transmittal should be attached to the outside of the inner wrapper of the package containing the evidence. In this connection it is pointed out that it is extremely desirable to individually wrap and identify each item of evidence being forwarded and these individual items should be included in a package which is wrapped and sealed. To the outside of this wrapping should be affixed a copy of the letter of transmittal. Thereafter, the entire package should be again wrapped with a shipping wrapper and the necessary labels for shipment attached to this package. The use of registered mail or registered air mail is appropriate for most items weighing less than four pounds. Such items as live ammunition, explosives, bottles of corrosive liquids and acids may not be shipped by this method. Firearms, however, may be shipped by this manner provided the package is labeled, "Firearms, Official Law Enforcement Shipment."

Items which cannot be economically, or by reason of shipping restrictions, shipped by regular methods may be forwarded Railway Express or Air Express marked, "Special Handling" to insure safe transit. The "Special Handling" service is comparable to the security afforded by the use of registered mail in the postal service. In all cases live ammunition, explosives, inflammables, acids, and other corrosive chemicals must be shipped in this manner. It is pointed out, however, that under no circumstances should explosive materials be forwarded to the FBI Laboratory without prior instructions from this Bureau as to the proper method of packing and shipping. Instructions concerning the shipment of this material may be obtained by telephone, telegraph, or letter, depending upon the circumstances.

(3) *Personal delivery.*—In emergency situations evidence will be accepted in the FBI Laboratory when delivered personally by a law enforcement officer. When this method is used it is helpful if a letter outlining the circumstances of the case and following in general the outline form set forth under the heading "Letter of Transmittal" accompanies the evidence.

Return shipments from the FBI Laboratory are made by registered mail when possible. All other shipments are made by railway or air express collect.

FBI Laboratory Procedure

The following information is set forth as of possible assistance in understanding the administrative procedure followed in the FBI Laboratory in the assignment, examination and return of evidence specimens:

When a letter of transmittal is received a determination is made from this letter as to what examinations will be required and an examiner is assigned to make the examination. If the shipment has been made "under separate cover," the package is delivered to the FBI Laboratory unopened and the letter of transmittal is associated with this package. The association of the package with the original letter of transmittal is speeded by incorporation of a copy of the letter inside the wrapper of the package as outlined above. When the letter and package are associated with each other they are then delivered to the examiner who will make the examinations. It is his responsibility to check the contents of the package against the contents as listed in the letter of transmittal. When this check has been completed, a letter of acknowledgment is prepared advising the contributing agency that the evidence has been received and a report will be forthcoming. In the event certain essential information required in the proper indexing or examination of the case has been overlooked in the letter of transmittal, this additional information will be requested in the letter of acknowledgment. The information asked for in this letter is essential and the investigator's cooperation in promptly furnishing the additional information required is helpful.

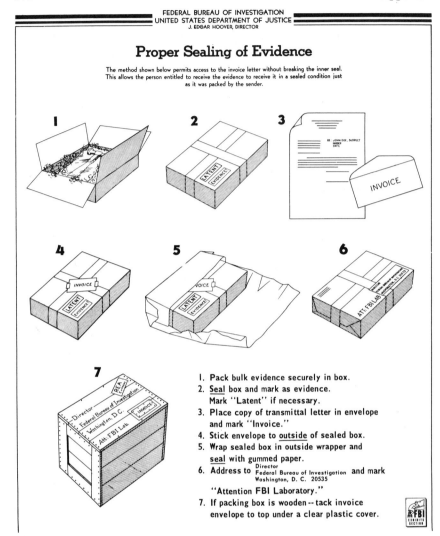

FEDERAL BUREAU OF INVESTIGATION
UNITED STATES DEPARTMENT OF JUSTICE
J. EDGAR HOOVER, DIRECTOR

Proper Sealing of Evidence

The method shown below permits access to the invoice letter without breaking the inner seal. This allows the person entitled to receive the evidence to receive it in a sealed condition just as it was packed by the sender.

1. Pack bulk evidence securely in box.
2. Seal box and mark as evidence. Mark "Latent" if necessary.
3. Place copy of transmittal letter in envelope and mark "Invoice."
4. Stick envelope to outside of sealed box.
5. Wrap sealed box in outside wrapper and seal with gummed paper.
6. Address to Director Federal Bureau of Investigation Washington, D. C. 20535 and mark "Attention FBI Laboratory."
7. If packing box is wooden -- tack invoice envelope to top under a clear plastic cover.

Figure 75.

At the time the items of evidence are checked against those listed in the letter of transmittal, specimen numbers are assigned for ease in future reference. The FBI Laboratory uses a system of "Q" and "K" numbers for this purpose. It is suggested that contributors not attempt to assign "Q" or "K" numbers to the items of evidence being submitted. This will avoid conflict and confusion between the numbers assigned by the contributor and those assigned in the Laboratory. It has been found most desirable for the contributor to identify his evidence simply by items numbered 1, 2, 3, 4, etc.

Following the verification of the evidence with the letter of transmittal a work sheet is prepared listing the various items of evidence submitted and setting forth the other administrative details required in the proper handling of the case. Upon this sheet are placed the technical findings of the examiner. This sheet, therefore, contains the original notes of the examination performed and will later be used by the examiner during future examinations in this case or when testifying.

Upon completion of the examination, the examiner prepares a report setting forth results of the various examinations conducted. Following the preparation of the report, the evidence specimens are wrapped for shipment. The evidence return is affected by one of the methods set forth above.

Bulky Evidence and Test Specimens

Where large pieces of evidence are submitted for examination, such as safe doors, much time may be saved if the submitting agency will grant permission for removal of portions of the evidence bearing significant areas for study. Many times examinations under the microscope are necessary but due to the bulky nature of the material, such examinations are not possible unless the bulky items can be reduced to convenient size.

When an unusual type of material is recovered and comparative tests are requested, material should be included with the specimens which can be used for test purposes. Occasionally sufficient material is available on the evidence specimens, but here again it is desirable to include a statement to the effect that test material is included or test material may be obtained from the evidence specimens submitted.

Check the Evidence Returned

When the evidence is returned to the contributor, the package should be opened and the individual items contained therein compared with the listing contained in the letter of transmittal, as well as those items listed in the laboratory report. It is desirable that the opening and checking of these specimens be handled by the officer who prepared the material for shipment to the FBI Laboratory. This procedure will reduce the number of persons required to testify at the trial concerning the custody of the items introduced as evidence.

The FBI Laboratory should be advised immediately of any discrepancies between the items forwarded for examination and the items returned. Where differences occur, extreme care should be exercised in examining all of the packing material utilized in the shipment in order that the missing items will not be inadvertently disposed of with this material.

After a complete accounting of each item has been made, the box should be resealed and thereafter retained in a safe and secure place to insure against tampering or unauthorized handling.

Testimony at the Trial

At the time of the trial the items of physical evidence to be introduced will be decided upon by the prosecuting attorney. He is responsible for the proper introduction of the various items of physical evidence. During the trial procedure any mistakes or errors in the collection and preservation of the items of evidence may be greatly emphasized by the defense counsel.

The witness, however, should not become unduly concerned in this connection if the proper procedures have been followed in the identification and preservation of each item of evidence. If these procedures have been adhered to, the testimony of each witness will assist in the welding of an unbroken chain of evidence.

Witnesses should never be hasty in the identification of the various items of evidence presented to them on the witness stand. The identification marks placed on each item should be carefully observed and positively identified before the identification of the specimen is established. Faulty identifications and ambiguous answers nullify the effects of otherwise pertinent and important testimony.

During this testimony the identity marks used by the investigator prove their worth. Fortified with notes prepared during the course of his investigation, the witness is prepared to describe in detail what was found, where it was found and the conditions surrounding the recovery. Here as in no other situation the value of complete and well organized notes is demonstrated.

The testimony concerning the physical evidence in many cases forms the very heart of a successful prosecution. Unquestionably facts developed from the examination of these items demand and receive the profound attention of all jurors provided the presentation and interpretation of the facts are properly and fairly made.

There should be no "fumbling" or guesswork during the investigator's testimony. Each must provide his link to complete the "chain of evidence." In the absence of one link in the chain or some "slip up" in the ground work preparatory to offering an exhibit in evidence, the court has no alternative but to exclude that item of physical evidence. The result of such a ruling is plain to see. Measures to prevent such happenings lie in proper training and in the acceptance by the investigator of the tremendous responsibilities which attach themselves to law enforcement work.

Expert Testimony

Special agents of the FBI Laboratory will be made available to testify in those cases where examinations have been performed provided no other expert in the same scientific field will be used by the prosecution. This policy is in harmony with the restrictions placed upon FBI Laboratory examinations concerning duplication of effort. This testimony is given at no cost to the State, county or municipal governments.

In those cases where FBI Laboratory examinations have been performed, essential testimony may be obtained by addressing a letter to "Director, Federal Bureau of Investigation, U.S. Department of Justice, Washington 25, D.C." In view of the circumstances surrounding the testimony, it can be appreciated that every effort should be made to utilize the services of these witnesses as quickly as possible, consistent with good trial procedures, and to arrange for their immediate release following court appearance.

In most cases the presence of an expert witness is not required by the court during the jury selection and, consequently, he need not be present when the case is called. It is usually possible to anticipate when the expert testimony will be required and arrangements can be made to have the witness present at that time.

In order to complete the case file in those cases where testimony has been given by FBI Laboratory personnel, a letter from the investigating agency or the attorney representing the people, setting forth the findings of the court together with the sentence imposed, will be appreciated.

Conclusion

A review of the essential elements of identification, preservation, examination, and court presentation with respect to physical evidence as brought together here graphically demonstrates the relationship of one step to the other. One can readily appreciate that each step in this procedure has a direct bearing on the conviction of the guilty or the acquittal of the innocent. That achievement is the ultimate goal of every criminal investigation. The deftness with which each step has been executed can be directly correlated with the thoroughness of the basic training provided the new police officer as well as the experienced investigator. These problems present a challenge to every member of the profession.

Suggestions for Handling Physical Evidence

CHART TO BE USED IN SUBMITTING EVIDENCE
TO THE FBI LABORATORY

This chart is not intended to be all-inclusive. If evidence to be submitted is not found herein, consult the specimen list for an item most similar in nature and submit accordingly.

Specimen	Identification	Amount Desired Standard	Evidence
Abrasives, including carborundum, emery, sand, etc.	On outside of container. Type of material. Date obtained. Name or initials.	Not less than one ounce	All
Acids	Same as above	One pint	All to one pint
Adhesive tape	Same as above	Recovered roll	All
Alkalies—caustic soda, potash, ammonia, etc.	Same as above	One pint liquid / One pound solid	All to one pint / All to one pound
Ammunition	Same as above	Two	
Anonymous letters, extortion letters, bank robbery notes	Initial and date each document unless legal aspects or good judgment dictates otherwise.		All
Blasting caps	On outside of container. Type of material, date obtained, and name or initials.		All

eservation	Wrapping and Packing	Transmittal	Miscellaneous
ıe	Use containers, such as ice-cream box, pillbox, or plastic vial. Seal to prevent any loss.	Registered mail or RR or air express	Avoid use of envelopes.
ıe	Plastic or all-glass bottle. Tape in stopper. Pack in sawdust, glass, or rock wool. Use bakelite- or paraffin-lined bottle for hydrofluoric acid.	RR express only	Label acids, glass, corrosive.
ıe	Place on waxed paper or cellophane.	Registered mail	Do not cut, wad, or distort.
ıe	Plastic or glass bottle with rubber stopper held with adhesive tape	RR express only	Label alkali, glass, corrosive.
ne	Pack in cotton, soft paper, or cloth in small container. Place in wooden box.	RR express only	If standard make, usually not necessary to send. Explosive label.
not handle vith bare ıands.	Place in proper enclosure envelope and seal with "Evidence" tape or transparent cellophane tape. Flap side of envelope should show (1) wording "Enclosure(s) to Bureau from (name of submitting office)," (2) title of case, (3) brief description of contents, and (4) file number, if known. Staple to original letter of transmittal.	Registered mail	Advise if evidence should be treated for latent fingerprints.

ould not be forwarded until advised to do so by the Laboratory. Packing instructions
will be given at that time.

Specimen	Identification	Amount Desired Standard	Eviden
Blood:			
1. Liquid Known samples	Use adhesive tape on outside of test tube. Name of donor, date taken, doctor's name, name or initials of submitting Agent or officer.	⅙ ounce (5cc) collected in sterile test tube	All
2. Drowning cases	Same as above	Two specimens: one from each side of heart	
3. Small quantities: a. Liquid Questioned samples	Same as above as applicable		All to ⅙ ounce (5cc)
b. Dry stains Not on fabrics	On outside of pillbox or plastic vial. Type of specimen, date secured, name or initials.		As much as possib
4. Stained clothing, fabric, etc.	Use tag or mark directly on clothes. Type of specimens, date secured, name or initials.		As found
Bullets (not cartridges)	Initials on base		All found
Cartridges	Initials on outside of case near bullet end	Two	
Cartridge cases (shells)	Initials preferably on inside near open end or on outside near open end.		All

eservation	Wrapping and Packing	Transmittal	Miscellaneous
le tube ly. *No eservative. No frigerant.*	Wrap in cotton, soft paper. Place in mailing tube or suitably strong mailing carton.	Airmail, special delivery, registered	Submit immediately. Don't hold awaiting additional items for comparison.
e as above	Same as above	Airmail, special delivery, registered	Same as above
w to dry oroughly n nonporous rface.	Same as above	Airmail, special delivery, registered	Collect by using eyedropper or clean spoon, transfer to nonporous surface. Allow to dry and submit in pillbox.
p dry.	Seal to prevent leakage.	Registered mail	
et when und, dry y hanging. SE NO EAT TO RY. No eservative.	Each article wrapped separately and identified on outside of package. Place in strong box packed to prevent shifting of contents.	Registered mail or air or RR express	
e	Place in cotton or soft paper. Place in pill, match, or powder box. Pack to prevent shifting during transit.	Registered mail	
e	Same as above	RR express only	
e	Same as above	Registered mail	

Specimen	Identification	Amount Desired Standard	Eviden*
Charred or burned paper	On outside of container indicate fragile nature of evidence, date obtained, name or initials.		All
Checks (fraudulent)	See anonymous letters.		All
Check protector, rubber stamp and dater stamp sets, known standards Note: Send actual device when possible.	Place name or initials, date, name of make and model, etc., on sample impressions.	Obtain several copies in full word-for-word order of each questioned check-writer impression. If unable to forward rubber stamps, prepare numerous samples with different degrees of pressure.	
Clothing	Mark directly on garment or use string tag. Type of evidence, name or initials, date.		All
Codes, ciphers, and foreign language material	As anonymous letters		All

Preservation	Wrapping and Packing	Transmittal	Miscellaneous
None	Pack in rigid container between layers of cotton.	Registered mail	Added moisture, with atomizer or otherwise, not recommended
None	See anonymous letters.	Registered mail	Advise what parts questioned or known. Furnish physical description of subject.
None	See anonymous letters or bulky evidence wrapping instructions.	Registered mail	Do not disturb inking mechanisms on printing devices
None	Each article individually wrapped with identification written on outside of package. Place in strong container.	Registered mail or RR or air express	Leave clothing whole. Do not cut out stains. If wet, hang in room to dry before packing.
None	As anonymous letters	As anonymous letters	Furnish all background and technical information pertinent to examination.

Specimen	Identification	Standard	Evidence
			Amount Desired
Drugs: 1. Liquids	Affix label to bottle in which found including name or initials and date.		All to one pint
2. Powders, pills, and solids	On outside of pillbox. Name or initials and date.		All to ¼ pound
Dynamite and other explosives	Consult the FBI Laboratory and follow their telephonic or telegraphic instructions.		
Fibers	On outside of sealed container or on object to which fibers are adhering	Entire garment or other cloth item	All
Firearms	Attach string tag. Name of weapons, caliber, serial number, date found, name or initials. Serial number in notes.		All
Flash paper	Initials and date	One sheet	All
Fuse, safety	Attach string tag or gummed paper label, name or initials, and date.	One foot	All

190

Preservation	Wrapping and Packing	Transmittal	Miscellaneous
one	If bottle has no stopper, transfer to glass-stoppered bottle and seal with adhesive tape.	Registered mail or RR or air express	Mark "Fragile." Determine alleged normal use of drug and if prescription, check with druggist to determine supposed ingredients.
one	Seal to prevent any loss by use of tape.	Registered mail or RR or air express	
one	Folded paper or pillbox. Seal edges and openings with tape.	Registered mail	Do not place loose in envelope.
eep from rusting.	Wrap in paper and identify contents of package. Place in cardboard box or wooden box.	Registered mail or RR or air express	Unload all weapons before shipping.
ireproof, vented location away from any other combustible materials. If feasible, immerse in water.	Individual polyethylene envelopes double wrapped in manila envelopes. Inner wrapper sealed with paper tape.	Five sheets (8 x 10½) surface mail parcel post. Over 5 sheets telephonically consult FBI Laboratory.	Mark inner wrapper "Flash Paper Flammable."
one	Place in manila envelope, box, or suitable container.	Registered mail or RR or air express	

		Amount Desired	
Specimen	Identification	Standard	Evidenc
Gasoline	On outside of all-metal container, label with type of material, name or initials and date.	One quart	All to on gallon
Glass fragments	Adhesive tape on each piece. Name or initials and date on tape. Separate questioned and known.		All
Glass particles	Name or initials, date on outside of sealed container	3" piece of broken item	All
Gunpowder tests: 1. Paraffin	On outside of container, Type of material, date, and name or initials.		All
2. On cloth	Attach string tag or mark directly. Type of material, date, and name or initials.		All
Hair	On outside of container. Type of material, date, and name or initials.	Dozen or more full length hairs from different parts of head and / or body	All
Handwriting and hand printing, known standards	Name or initials, date, from whom obtained, and voluntary statement should be included in appropriate place.	See footnote.°	

° Duplicate the original writing conditions as to text, speed, slant, size of paper, size of writing, type of writing instruments, etc. Do not allow suspect to see questioned writing. Give no instructions as to spelling, punctuation, etc. Remove each sample from sight as soon as completed. Suspect should fill out blank check forms in cases (FD-352). In hand printing cases, both upper- (capital) and lo er-case (small) samples should be obtain In forgery cases, obtain sample signatures the person whose name is forged. H writer prepare some specimens with hand normally used. Obtain undictated handw ing when feasible.

Preservation	Wrapping and Packing	Transmittal	Miscellaneous
Fireproof container	Metal container packed in wooden box	RR express only	
Avoid chipping.	Wrap each piece separately in cotton. Pack in strong box to prevent shifting and breakage. Identify contents.	Registered mail or RR or air express	Mark "Fragile."
None	Place in pillbox, plastic or glass vial; seal and protect against breakage.	Registered mail	Do not use envelopes.
Containers must be free of any nitrate-containing substance. Keep cool.	Wrap in waxed paper or place in sandwich bags. Lay on cotton in a substantial box. Place in a larger box packed with absorbent material.	Registered mail	Use "Fragile" label. Keep cool.
None	Place fabric flat between layers of paper and then wrap, so that no residue will be transferred or lost.	Registered mail	Avoid shaking.
None	Folded paper or pillbox. Seal edges and openings with tape.	Registered mail	Do not place loose in envelope.
None	See anonymous letters.	Registered mail	

Specimen	Identification	Amount Desired Standard	Evidence
Matches	On outside of container. Type of material, date, and name or initials.	One to two books of paper. One full box of wood.	All
Medicines (See drugs.)			
Metal	Same as above	One pound	All to one pound
Oil	Same as above	One quart together with specifications	All to one quart
Obliterated, eradicated, or indented writing	See anonymous letters.		All
Organs of body	On outside of container. Victim's name, date of death, date of autopsy, name of doctor, name or initials.		All to one pound
Paint: 1. Liquid	On outside of container. Type of material, origin if known, date, name or initials.	Original unopened container up to 1 gallon if possible	All to $\frac{1}{4}$ pint

Preservation	Wrapping and Packing	Transmittal	Miscellaneous
eep away from fire.	Metal container and packed in larger package to prevent shifting. Matches in box or metal container packed to prevent friction between matches.	RR express or registered mail	"Keep away from fire" label
eep from rusting.	Use paper boxes or containers. Seal and use strong paper or wooden box.	Registered mail or RR or air express	Melt number, heat treatment. and other specifications of foundry if available
eep away from fire.	Metal container with tight screw top. Pack in strong box using excelsior or similar material.	RR express only	DO NOT USE DIRT OR SAND FOR PACKING MATERIAL.
one	See anonymous letters.	Registered mail	Advise whether bleaching or staining methods may be used. Avoid folding.
one to evidence. Dry ice in package not touching glass jars.	Plastic or all-glass containers (glass jar with glass top)	RR or air express	"Fragile" label. Keep cool. Metal top containers must not be used. Send autopsy report.
one	Friction-top paint can or large-mouth, screw-top jars. If glass, pack to prevent breakage. Use heavy corrugated paper or wooden box.	Registered mail or RR or air express	

| Specimen | Identification | Amount Desired | |
		Standard	Evidence
2. Solid (paint chips or scrapings)	Same as above	At least ½ sq. inch of solid, with all layers represented	All. If on small object send object.
Plaster casts of tire treads and shoe prints	On back before plaster hardens. Location, date, and name or initials.	Send in shoes and tires of suspects. Photographs and sample impressions are usually not suitable for comparison.	All shoe prints; entire circumference of tires.
Powder patterns (See gunpowder tests.)			
Rope, twine, and cordage	On tag or container. Type of material, date, name or initials.	One yard	All
Safe insulation or soil	On outside of container. Type of material, date, name or initials.	½ pound	All to one pound
Shoe print lifts (impressions on hard surfaces)	On lifting tape or paper attached to tape. Name or initials and date.	Photograph before making lift of dust impression.	All
Tools	On tools or use string tag. Type of tool, identifying number, date, name or initials.		All

Preservation	Wrapping and Packing	Transmittal	Miscellaneous
Wrap so as to protect smear.	If small amount, round pillbox or small glass vial with screw top. Seal to prevent leakage. Envelopes not satisfactory.	Registered mail or RR or air express	Do not pack in cotton. Avoid contact with adhesive materials.
Allow casts to cure (dry) before wrapping.	Wrap in paper and cover with suitable packing material to prevent breakage. Do not wrap in unventilated plastic bags.	Registered mail or RR or air express	Use "Fragile" label. Mix approximately four pounds of plaster to quart of water.
	Wrap securely.	Registered mail	
	Use containers, such as pillbox, or plastic vial. Seal to prevent any loss.	Registered mail or RR or air express	Avoid use of glass containers and envelopes.
None	Prints in dust are easily damaged. Fasten print or lift to bottom of a box so that nothing will rub against it.	Registered mail	Always rope off crime scene area until shoe prints or tire treads are located and preserved.
	Wrap each tool in paper. Use strong cardboard or wooden box with tools packed to prevent shifting.	Registered mail or RR or air express	

		Amount Desired	
Specimen	Identification	Standard	Evidence
Toolmarks	On object or on tag attached to or on opposite end from where toolmarks appear. Name or initials and date.	Send in the tool. If impractical, make several impressions on similar material as evidence using entire marking area of tool.	All
Typewriting, known standards	Place name or initials, date, serial number, name of make and model, etc., on specimens.	Obtain at least one copy in full word-for-word order of questioned typewriting. Also include partial copies in light, medium, and heavy degrees of touch. Also carbon paper samples of every character on the keyboard.	
Urine or water	On outside of container. Type of material, name of subject, date taken, name or initials.	Preferably all urine voided over a period of 24 hours	All
Wire (See also toolmarks.)	On label or tag. Type of material, date, name or initials.	Three feet (Do not kink.)	All (Do not kink.)
Wood	Same as above	One foot	All

Preservation	Wrapping and Packing	Transmittal	Miscellaneous
Cover ends bearing toolmarks with soft paper and wrap with strong paper to protect ends.	After marks have been protected, wrap in strong wrapping paper, place in strong box, and pack to prevent shifting.	Registered mail or RR or air express	
None	See anonymous letters.	Registered mail	Examine ribbon for evidence of questioned message thereon. For carbon paper samples either remove ribbon or place in stencil position.
None. Use any clean bottle with leakproof stopper.	Bottle surrounded with absorbent material to prevent breakage. Strong cardboard or wooden box.	Registered mail	
	Wrap securely.	Registered mail	Do not kink wire.
	Wrap securely.	Registered mail	

Index

Other Books in the Inbau Law Enforcement Series

Criminal Law for the Police,
                by Fred E. Inbau and Marvin E. Aspen

Criminal Law for the Layman,
                by Fred E. Inbau and Marvin E. Aspen

Fingerprints and The Law,
                by Andre A. Moenssens

Fingerprint Techniques
                by Andre A. Moenssens

Evidence Law for the Police
                by Fred E. Inbau, Marvin E. Aspen and
                Frank Carrington

About the Authors

FRED E. INBAU is Professor of Law at Northwestern University and was formerly Director of the Chicago Police Scientific Crime Detection Laboratory. He is the author of numerous books and articles about criminal investigation and criminal law and is former editor of the *Journal of Criminal Law, Criminology and Police Science*.

ANDRE A. MOENSSENS is Associate Professor of Law at the Chicago-Kent College of Law of the Illinois Institute of Technology and founder of the school's Institute for Criminal Justice. An authority on fingerprinting, he has been associate editor of *Finger Print and Identification Magazine* and is the author of two definitive books on the subject. He was one of the two fingerprint experts who testified at the 1967 Speck murder trial.

LOUIS R. VITULLO, who has served in the laboratory of the Chicago Police Department since 1953, is Chief Microanalyst of its Criminalistics Division.